D1110600

WHO CALLS ME
Beautiful?

Discovery House Publishers

Books, music, and videos that feed the soul with the Word of God

Box 3566 Grand Rapids, MI 49501

WHO CALLS ME
Beautiful?

Finding Our True Image
in the Mirror of God

REGINA FRANKLIN

Library of Congress Cataloging-in-Publication Data
Franklin, Regina.
    Who calls me beautiful? : Finding our true image in the mirror of God /
by Regina Franklin.
      p. cm.
    ISBN 1-57293-125-6
    1. Women--Religious life. [1. Beauty, Personal--Religious
aspects--Christianity.] I. Title.
    BV4527.F735 2004
    248.8'43--dc22
                            2004007758

Printed in the United States of America

04 05 06 07 08 09 10 / DP / 10 9 8 7 6 5 4 3 2

To Scott—
for being a man of God
and for seeing God's beauty in me.

··· CONTENTS ···

 ORLDLY BEAUTY

W HEN I was a child, beauty pageants mesmerized me
with their depictions of glamour. I imagined myself dancing
and singing like the women I saw on the television screen,
and I longed to be one of them.

Every little girl imagines herself as the star of her own
show, the princess in her own kingdom. These dreams of
childhood dwell deep within us. But at some point we learn
to distinguish reality from illusion.

For some reason, however, the beauty myth lingers long
after childhood days pass. Our fascination with the
beautiful princess myth is especially problematic because it
turns simple character description into the dominating
theme. Physical beauty becomes the message of life's story
rather than a mere detail. Stories about love so strong that it
risks danger to rescue the beloved are reduced to stories of

maidens worth rescuing only because of their exceptional beauty. Certainly not a message of destiny. Certainly not a message of hope. Yet we live every day in a world that tells us physical beauty reigns in the kingdom of popular culture.

Ironically, women have been able to see and reject the 1950s illusion of June Cleaver's moral perfection. But when it comes to the illusion of physical perfection, women long to achieve it, no matter how unattainable.

Our admiration for the inhabitants of Hollywood rarely has to do with their acting ability. Riveted to pictures of glamour striding across red carpet, we convince ourselves that happiness and success are awarded exclusively to those who attain beauty.

Whether I'm clipping coupons, reading the paper, or searching for information online, I am bombarded by advertisements carrying the elusive promise of a thinner, newer, better me. From commercials to sitcoms, thin bodies dominate the television airwaves.

In his article "What You See Is What I Am," youth culture expert Walt Mueller wrote,

> Our entire culture—children and adults alike—is living a lifestyle that screams, "I am what I look like." A walk through any shopping mall confirms this fact. Have you noticed how many businesses, advertisements, and items of merchandise are sold to improve image and appearance?[1]

Hair products promise to give more bounce to curls or remove unwanted curl. Skin products promise blemish-free skin when we're young and wrinkle-free skin when we're old. We are obsessed with self-dissatisfaction.

Daily, we face the onslaught of pictures of cultural perfection. Gradually, the images become our reality. We lose sight of the fact that the pictures were created to sell products. Desiring acceptance from the world, we undertake any number of measures to look like the world says we should look. From endless diets to radical and cosmetic surgeries, creams to pills, clothes to shoes, we keep trying to recreate ourselves in the world's image of perfection. Unable to end this futile pursuit, we become like the man in Stephen Crane's poem:

> I saw a man pursuing the horizon;
> Round and round they sped.
> I was disturbed at this;
> I accosted the man.
> "It is futile," I said,
> "You can never—"
> "You lie," he cried,
> And ran on.[2]

The emotional emptiness that persists tells us that we are more than just physical beings. It insists that our value comes from more than physical appearance. But our inability to satisfy our longings convinces us that the promise of something more is a lie, and so we run on.

Even if we get close to achieving the cultural standard of beauty, the definition is likely to change. In her book *Reviving Ophelia*, Dr. Mary Pipher wrote,

> The right look has always mattered, but now it's harder to obtain. . . . The standards of beauty are more stringent. Miss Americas have become taller and slimmer over the years. In 1951, Miss Sweden was 5 feet 7 inches tall and weighed 151 pounds. In 1983, Miss Sweden was 5 feet 9 inches tall and 109 pounds. While beautiful women are slimmer, average women are heavier than they were in the 1950s. Thus the discrepancy between the real and the ideal is greater.[3]

Deeply concerned over the culture's portrayal of women, Pipher also believes we must recognize what she terms the "artifice" of the cultural standard of beauty:

> What is culturally accepted as beautiful is achieved only with great artifice—photo croppings, camera angles and composite bodies are necessary to get the pictures we now see of beautiful women. Even the stars cannot meet our cultural ideals without great costs.[4]

Patricia Heaton, co-star of the sitcom *Everybody Loves Raymond*, plays the role of ordinary housewife Debra Barone. Her body, however, is anything but ordinary. In an interview with writer Alex Witchel, Heaton talked openly about her much-publicized plastic surgery which "included a tummy tuck (much needed, she says, after her four sons were all delivered by caesarean) and an accompanying breast lift." Exemplifying the media's obsession with artificial beauty, and seeming to justify Heaton's choice, Witchel noted, "She really does look terrific, thin and toned."

Later in the interview, while discussing her various surgeries, Heaton pulled "from her purse a small plastic bag marked 'Lunch,' filled with pills and capsules. 'Herbs,' she says, 'something that helps process body fat, another that's an appetite suppressant.'"[5]

While acknowledging that her experience is not that of the average woman, Heaton continues to perpetuate the unattainable ideal through her own pursuit of physical perfection. Meanwhile, in her television role, she continues to portray an average housewife. Thus, the entertainment industry sends contradictory messages. While claiming to portray the average woman, it presents instead the culture's idea of the perfect woman.

Women strive to shape their lives after that which popular culture tells them is beautiful, and Christian women are no exception. When we are preoccupied with physical attractiveness, we assert that the world's standards of beauty matter more than God's, and we begin to reflect the values of a world that Jesus said we are not a part of even though we remain in it.

> "I do not pray that You should take them out of the world, but that You should keep them from the evil one. They are not of the world, just as I am not of the world." (John 17:15–16)

But what is in the world that we're not to be part of? Scripture gives the answer: "For all that is in the world—the lust of the flesh, the lust of the eyes, and the pride of life—is not of the Father but is of the world" (1 John 2:16).

THE LUST OF THE FLESH. Flip through most women's magazines and you'll see that our society focuses on the flesh—literally and figuratively. Women's faces and bodies dominate marketing campaigns, promoting everything from cars to candy. The message? Beauty equals satisfaction.

When Eve looked at the fruit growing on the tree of the knowledge of good and evil, she saw that it "was good for food" (Genesis 3:6). Even though God had warned that eating the fruit would result in spiritual destruction, Eve insisted on fulfilling the desire of her flesh.

Since then, Satan has continued to set before us the illusionary fruit of satisfaction. But to eat of such fruit is to sever our communion with God, for we are to live by and satisfy ourselves with *"every word that proceeds from the mouth of God"* (Matthew 4:4b, italics added).

THE LUST OF THE EYES. *The New Bible Commentary* defines the lust of the eyes as a "strong desire for what is seen, for the outward form of things. It is the lust after the superficial."[6]

In the second temptation, Satan urged Jesus to throw Himself down from the highest point of the temple (Matthew 4:6) to test the Scripture: "He shall give His angels charge over you. . . . [T]hey shall bear you up, lest you dash your foot against a stone" (Psalm 91:11–12).

God gave these words as a promise of His abiding

provision and protection. Satan, however, wanted Jesus to claim the promise to further Satan's purpose rather than God's. He intended to misappropriate God's gift of divine protection and use it to bring glory to himself.

In much the same way, Satan wants to misuse God's gift of our bodies for his purposes rather than God's.

We live in a visual culture—images elicit responses. When we strive to meet the world's standard of beauty, our bodies become images to evoke desired responses within ourselves and others. When we mold ourselves according to the world's image, we take what God has created to be a vessel of His glory and use it instead to glorify ourselves and satisfy our desire for admiration.

Efforts to have a beautiful face and body rarely come from the desire to reflect more accurately the body of Christ. Rather, they have roots in the desire to make ourselves "pleasant to the eyes" (Genesis 3:6).

Worldly beauty is a means to an end, a way of gaining a positive response to ourselves from someone other than God. However, having been created in the image of God, we are to use our bodies as a witness for the kingdom of God.

THE PRIDE OF LIFE. In the third and final temptation, Satan offered Jesus "all the kingdoms of the world and their glory" if Jesus would worship Satan (Matthew 4:8–9).

Satan's offer to women is similar: "Bow down to the god of beauty and I will give you power."

Women desire beauty because the world says it brings power and control. Like little girls who believe the illusions of beauty pageants, we believe that women who look perfect have achieved power over themselves and others, a power we all want to possess.

However, believing the myth that beauty will empower us is nothing more than desiring "all the kingdoms of the world and their glory."

Nineteenth-century British poet William Wordsworth, frustrated by the pursuit of materialism in his society, wrote a poem that also relates to the pursuit of beauty in our own:

> The world is too much with us; late and soon,
> Getting and spending, we lay waste our powers:
> Little we see in Nature that is ours;
> We have given our hearts away, a sordid boon! (1–4).[7]

Believing the world's definition of beauty, we too "have given our hearts away."

Within me, however, lives an insatiable and tenacious longing to be free from the world's standard of beauty. The very existence of this longing tells me there is something more to who I am than the ideal I've been chasing.

Little girls dream, and little girls grow up. The deepest longing of my grown-up heart is to be known as a woman of God—to my husband, to my children, to the world around me.

Beyond the dreams and illusions of childhood is One who calls me beautiful. His voice never falters, never ceases, even when I continue my childhood games, even when I keep listening to voices other than His.

LOOKING IN THE MIRROR
Personal Reflection

What images of beauty captured your attention as a child? What is your perception of these images today?

The apostle Paul wrote: "When I was a child, I spoke as a child, I understood as a child, I thought as a child; but when I became a man, I put away childish things" (1 Corinthians 13:11). In what ways have you held onto a "childish" understanding of beauty?

Consider 1 John 2:16: "For all that is in the world—the lust of the flesh, the lust of the eyes, and the pride of life—is not of the Father but is of the world."

Lust of the Flesh. Give three examples of advertisements that use a woman's face or body to sell their products. What promises do these products offer? How realistically can the product fulfill such a promise?

What message does the use of women in advertising communicate to men? How do these images affect what men think of women and how they behave toward them? What examples of this type of response do you see in men and women you know?

Lust of the Eyes. In what ways do you use your body to bring glory or affirmation to yourself?

Why do you think women use their bodies to elicit a response from others?

Pride of Life. What messages do you attempt to send to others through your physical appearance? How do these messages line up with what God says about your body?

List three areas of physical beauty—according to the world's standard—that you feel you lack.

Analyze those three beauty stereotypes in light of Genesis 3:6: "So when the woman saw that the tree was good for food, that it was pleasant to the eyes, and a tree desirable to make one wise, she took of its fruit and ate. She also gave to her husband with her, and he ate."

In what ways do you think the stereotypes will bring you satisfaction (i.e., are "good for food")?

In what ways do the stereotypes ignore or distort God's plan for your body (i.e., what is "pleasant to the eyes") ?

In what ways do these stereotypes promote the idea that beauty equals knowledge and power (i.e., "make one wise")?

Identify one of your deep spiritual longings. Does your attitude toward your own physical beauty and your pursuit of the world's beauty help or hinder the fulfillment of this longing?

TWO

OICES WITHOUT

IN *The House on Mango Street*, author Sandra Cisneros depicts a young girl's coming of age. Esperanza, the protagonist in the story, and her two friends ponder the mysteries of womanhood while jumping rope. Modeling what they've learned from society, the young girls believe that adulthood comes with physical maturation. Welcoming the changes in their bodies, they believe that growing up will provide them with the answers to life's many questions and complexities. In childlike innocence, Esperanza describes a girl's hips as "bloom[ing] like roses." Giving her friends directions as to how to swing the jump rope, Esperanza advises, "Not too fast and not too slow. Not too fast and not too slow," unwittingly addressing not only the pace of the rope, but also the pace of a young girl growing up. As they continue their games, she and her two young friends sing a song in anticipation of the hips that they believe will make them women:

> Some are skinny like chicken lips.
> Some are baggy like soggy Band-Aids
> After you get out of the bathtub.
> I don't care what kind I get.
> Just as long as I get hips.[1]

As time progresses, however, Esperanza learns that becoming a woman physically begets more complexities.

Adolescence is a confusing, life-altering period of time. Most women remember the years not in terms of how beautiful they felt, but how awkward and insecure they believed themselves to be. But adolescence is also a pivotal period, for that is when a young woman defines her perceptions of beauty. Familiar rites of passage, while greatly anticipated, bring more questions than answers and often leave young girls wondering who they are and where they belong.

Pantyhose, bras, pierced earrings, and makeup. Markers of womanhood. My sister and I were allowed one rite of passage at a time—and only when my parents deemed the time appropriate, "not too fast and not too slow." The momentum of growing up increases with each rite of passage, and my parents wisely controlled the pace, much to the chagrin of my sister and me. But one thing my parents could not hold in check was the maturation of our bodies.

When I was young, I could hardly wait for my body to fill in. To me, the arrival of breasts and hips meant that I was that much closer to adulthood. But more changed during adolescence than just my body.

I began to hear clamoring voices of family and friends who unknowingly uttered statements that forever affected the way I perceived myself. Not all of the words were spoken. I understood even those left unspoken.

VOICES OF PEERS. Do you remember the day when you tucked away the things of childhood and reached out to the woman you were to become? No longer content to play with Barbie dolls, you wanted to be Barbie—the girl who could capture any young man's heart, who knew what she wanted out of life and knew how to get it, who knew the right thing to do and say in any situation, who always looked great and knew it.

Did you ever find her?

She was only a few years older than I, but we were light years apart. She was everything I wanted to be—tall, blond, confident, and beautiful. I found myself wishing away my short, awkward, insecure self. She was a model; I dreamed of looking like a model. She won the boy's heart; I dreamed of winning his *attention*. She was the center of the group; I dreamed of just being in the group. She was never unkind to me; she was just untouchable.

I was twelve years old, and my family had just moved from a small town in Minnesota to a suburb on the outskirts of Minneapolis where my dad had taken a new position at a different church.

Longing to belong, I quickly became involved in the church's youth group and sought out the friendships I so desired. But finding my place was much tougher than I had anticipated. Gone were the childhood games, and gone were the childhood friends. Adding struggle to difficulty, I was entering adolescence.

Church youth groups can be a place of spiritual training and healing; they can also be a gauntlet for a young woman's self-esteem.

I saw the way people sought the beautiful teenage girl, and their actions spoke volumes. The youth pastor's wife asked her advice on hair and makeup. The young men flocked to her side. The other girls wanted to be just like her. Her own sister called herself "the ugly one."

Time and distance, though, are great teachers. As I think back to those days, I suspect that even the beautiful teenage girl believed that she could never be enough. The one thing that she and all the other girls had in common was that each saw herself as too fat and never adequate. But at twelve years of age, and even later at sixteen, I didn't understand that despite the way things appeared, the girl I perceived as perfect didn't hold the world in the palm of her hand.

Instead, I too tried to be like her, and in doing so I wished away myself.

I knew I didn't measure up to the standard of beauty that all the girls were trying to attain, and something deep inside me knew I wasn't supposed to. One Sunday after church, I confided in the youth pastor's wife. Crying, I told her I was tired of feeling as if I had to call myself fat to fit in to their conversations. She acknowledged the truth in my words; but neither her life nor the lives of the girls in the youth group exhibited any change. Soon I too began to see myself as fat.

The changes I once so eagerly anticipated became my bane. I hated my young girl's body before it even finished developing, and I took up the mantra that marks so many women's conversations: "I'm so fat."

The voices I heard became my own.

THE VOICES OF FAMILY. Arriving on the front porch of my grandmother's house in my early teenage years, I was greeted by my uncle, "Your hips are wide enough to haul a trailer."

"How have you been?" just didn't suffice as a greeting in my family. Every time I visited my grandmother she told me I had hips like hers. To soften the sting, she would tell me her hips were what attracted my grandfather. But as I heard the way she talked about her own body, I knew her words were no compliment.

On both sides of my family, the women are well endowed. At any family gathering I could see my family heritage and my future inheritance in the breasts and hips around me. In my father's family, hips are thought to be more of a curse than a sign of womanhood, as they are generally broad and "baggy like soggy Band-Aids."

My grandmother still comments about my body whenever I visit. Taking her shopping on one particular visit, I stood with her in the pantyhose aisle at Kmart to help her find what she needed. As we selected the size and the color she wanted, she asked me what size pantyhose I wore. When I told her, she asked me if I could really fit into that size. Later, when I told her that I couldn't fit into the size six-and-one-half shoe that she was offering me, she said, "Why, Shug, your feet have gotten F-A-T."

When my sister and I visited her recently, we took our violins to practice for an upcoming wedding we were to play in. Since my father's death, my sister and I feel closest to him when we play our violins together. On this particular occasion, we wanted to share that experience with our grandmother.

As my sister and I stood in our father's childhood home, we longed for him again. We set our music on a chair against the wall and began to play. Memories of our dad played in our heads as we pulled our bows across the strings. Finishing the song, we looked at our grandmother, hoping to see the approval of our father in her eyes. Instead we saw her motioning with her hands how much our hips had grown.

To say that I miss my father deeply is to say that ocean water tastes slightly of salt. Without a doubt, he was one of the most influential forces in my life. He died of cancer shortly before he would have celebrated his fifty-first birthday. He was a man who knew how to create something out of nothing. From swimming in the "crick" behind his house to completing his PhD in music theory and composition, my father took the simplest of experiences and made them great.

The youngest son of a backwoods, small-town southern preacher, my father knew even as a young man that his dreams lay outside the boundaries of Vanceboro, North Carolina. So my father did what any young man does when he longs to see the world—he joined the Armed Forces. A gifted musician, he soon found his niche in an Air Force marching band.

My father was running from God when he left home, but he soon discovered that God could find him even outside of Vanceboro. He never had the opportunity to travel the world, but he discovered a greater desire and followed God's call into the ministry. He spent the next thirty-one years weaving the tapestry of his life from the fibers of his greatest loves—God, family, music, and learning.

Nothing but God can fill the void created by my father's death. But when I start dwelling on the loss of his presence, God reminds me to consider the gift of his life. He taught me the wonder of God and the wonder of learning, and he taught me that the two go hand in hand—to love God is to desire to know Him more.

Despite my father's many accomplishments, he was always frustrated with his physical appearance, especially his weight. He saw society's physical image of a successful man, and he allowed himself to be dwarfed by this standard. Thus, he lost sight of what made him truly valuable. While my father was a talented musician, a gifted teacher, and a trustworthy man, he struggled to comprehend his inherent value.

Though words were seldom spoken, he, too, heard "voices without" telling him that he didn't look the part of a minister. Seeing senior pastors validate men who appeared to be successful, and watching hiring committees choose staff based on physical appearance rather than on qualifications, my father heard the silent message loud and clear. A man's image indicates his value behind the pulpit.

Even though my father's genuineness drew people to him, he always shortchanged himself by thinking people wanted him to be someone different.

One of my father's few inconsistencies was that he rarely modeled what he told me regarding the relationship between achievement and self-esteem. The only thing my father expected of me was that I do my best. God would perform great works despite my weaknesses if I just did my best. However, I did not see this philosophy reflected in my father's perception of himself. His admonition to "Do as I say, not as I do" was insufficient to keep me from following his example and denigrating myself.

Negative ideas about himself permeated my father's speech, and I learned that same derogatory self-evaluation. My father chided me when he caught me belittling myself, but his behavior inadvertently (on his part and mine) became a part of me. After all, how could I find my appearance and achievements acceptable when the man whom I admired most found himself unacceptable?

From the time I was old enough to understand the meaning of the word *diet*, I heard the word often because it was a part my dad's everyday vocabulary. Accordingly, I grew up thinking yogurt, grapefruit, and Tab were staples in any successful weight-loss program. And for every new diet program, there was a new exercise regimen to match. Rockport tennis shoes for his new resolve to walk; bowling ball, shoes, and bag for the new sport he hoped to enjoy for exercise; and the small trampoline my sister and I enjoyed jumping on more than he. The only thing that lasted longer than my dad's diet and exercise programs was his desire to lose weight.

I also observed a troublesome element of my parents'
relationship: my father expected my mother to be guardian
of the refrigerator and thus the guardian of his dieting
destiny. I, too, found myself looking for someone to carry
the burden of my weight-loss, someone who not only would
help me lose weight but someone I could blame when I felt
fat.

One day as my parents sat talking at the kitchen table, I
marched resolutely into the room and announced that I
wanted them to monitor how many potato chips I was
eating. I was not overweight, nor were my eating habits
excessive. I was feeling ugly and unlovable, and I wanted
someone to help me change the outside of myself so I could
love the inside.

Wisely, my parents refused. At which point, I promptly
burst into tears and told them that if they wouldn't help
me, maybe I'd become bulimic or anorexic. Like my father, I
thought that controlling what I ate would produce the body
I wanted and the feeling of contentment that I longed for.
And like my father, I was missing the point.

My father passed away before I began to understand the
truth regarding self-image. He would have been deeply
grieved to know how intensely his self-perceptions affected
me. He thought his behavior affected only himself. But
speech that tears down one person's temple creates an
atmosphere, and all who enter feel its influence.

What voices do you hear from without? Childhood peers
whose taunts ring in your ears long after you've grown? A
parent whom you could never please and for whom you
never felt good enough? A husband who rarely tells you that

you're beautiful and whose silence echoes off the walls of your heart?

Hearing the voices, we search for ways to silence them. The diet that works, the perfect exercise program, a new hairstyle, a new makeover. Still, the voices linger, sometimes so loudly that we can barely hear the truth about ourselves.

I often wonder why my father couldn't see the incongruity of the world's definition of a man's value and his own God-given abilities. The more I think about this question, the more I realize that God's ideal for His creation will never match the world's—one relies upon the spirit of man as called out in faith by the omniscient and sovereign Creator of the universe while the other results from the manipulation and subsequent distortion of the spirit of man in order to appease a temporary and ephemeral world standard.

Such an incongruity is easy to overlook when we believe that if we could just fit society's image then everything else in life would fall into place. But a place of peace based on society's standards doesn't exist. On the contrary, the yearning to mirror society's image leaves us hungering for more. Because our self-esteem is rooted in our spirit, our longings to know who we are in Christ cannot be answered by countless diet and exercise programs in an attempt to remake our physical beings. Such a pursuit leaves our spiritual longing unanswered. Such a pursuit never silences the voices. Instead, the voices from without eventually are joined by the voices from within.

LOOKING IN THE MIRROR
Personal Reflection

What feelings come to mind when you
remember your adolescent years? Did
you feel confident about the woman
you were becoming?

What positive ideas did you form about womanhood during
adolescence? What forces helped to shape these positive
ideas?

When did your feelings toward your body become negative?

What role has your family played in shaping your
self-esteem? Be specific in identifying how family members'
words have affected you.

What other voices have impacted the way you view yourself
as a woman?

Look back at the spiritual longing that you identified in the
devotional for chapter one. How does your listening to the
voices around you hinder the fulfillment of this longing?

Take a moment to evaluate the words you speak, as well.
What does Matthew 12:36 say about our responsibility for
our words?

Scripture tells us that the power of life and death reside in the tongue (Proverbs 18:21a). Understanding this truth, we need to recognize that we have the power to speak life or death to those around us. Oftentimes, the voices that we hear affect more than just our lives; they affect the lives of all those we touch when we duplicate the same negative patterns of speech that we grew up hearing. If speaking negatively to or about others is an area with which you struggle, ask the Lord to place a guard over your mouth. If you are willing to listen to God's direction, He will give you the ability to begin speaking words of life to those around you.

One way to get Scripture from our minds to our hearts and into our lives is to savor it word by word. Savor the following Scriptures by writing them below or in a notebook.

Proverbs 25:11:

Colossians 4:6:

THREE

OICES WITHIN

CHOOSE any moment of any day and you can hear the cacophony of the world ringing in your ears. It's a wonder we can hear ourselves think, much less hear the voice of God.

Then come the voices with which we contend even in moments of solitude. These are voices within, the words we hear running through our heads in an endless diatribe.

Every woman hears them, but most feel helpless to silence them. Recognizing the power of the voices within, Nicole Johnson, author of *A Fresh Brewed Life* wrote,

> These voices keep our souls chained in the
> basement. They make us fearful to try anything
> new, anxious about what others think of us, and
> they keep us on the treadmill of performance.[1]

We have listened to these messages and obeyed them for so long that they have taken root in our hearts and become the words by which we live. Words of inadequacy, failure, ugliness. They are the lies that we know better than truth.

Ironically, when we feel the nagging desire to know beauty beyond this world, we hurriedly stifle these longings so as not to create any greater tension within us. What results is the masking of our true desires with a superficial sense of belonging.

T. S. Eliot's pre- and post-conversion poetry is as different as night and day. "The Love Song of J. Alfred Prufrock," one of his well-known pre-conversion works, aptly depicts the despondency of a man caught between the voices of the world and the voices within himself. Unable to break free from the expectations of society, and having nothing else to live for, Prufrock struggles with overwhelming indecision. While those around him idly enjoy their tea and conversation, Prufrock contemplates the pressure he feels to become someone different from who he is. In his endless inner dialogue, he agonizes,

> There will be time, there will be time
> To prepare a face to meet the faces that you meet;
> There will be time to murder and create.

When the voices without become the voices within, Prufrock believes that he must "murder" the truth of who he is in order to "create" himself in the image cast by society.

Prufrock's love song is a cry to be known by a world that imprisons him in superficiality. It is a world that pretends to know life while it withers in spiritual death. Considering this mundane and meaningless existence, Prufrock says,

> For I have known them all already, known them all—
> Have known the evenings, mornings, afternoons,
> I have measured out my life with coffee spoons;
> I know the voices dying with a dying fall
> Beneath the music from a farther room.

Something within him whispers that he was made for something more than isolation and rejection. However, unable to find his meaning and value apart from society, he is left with nothing. He closes out his mournful love song by saying,

> We have lingered in the chambers of the sea
> By sea-girls wreathed with seaweed red and brown
> Till human voices wake us, and we drown.[2]

Without hope, Prufrock drowns in the voices of despair within his own mind only to return to the deafening emptiness of the voices in the society that surrounds him.

Like Prufrock, the Christian woman hears the voices of society and the voices within her own heart and mind. Unlike Prufrock, however, she knows that true meaning comes from Someone outside of this world. She knows that true life is found in Christ. Often, however, she compartmentalizes her life. She can accept Christ as her righteousness in regard to her sin, but she has difficulty conceptualizing Christ as her beauty.

She lives with a divided heart, for she believes in Christ's ultimate love for her and yet feels burdened by her inability to love herself. Adding to her frustration, she fears that she is the only woman who struggles in this way, so she attempts to silence the voices. Her struggle becomes an issue of spiritual pride—an inability to allow Christ to be enough beauty for her and an unwillingness to allow others to see her insecurities.

Women learn early to play the games that hide their own fears of failure and feelings of inadequacy. Christian women are no different. Measuring our lives "with coffee spoons," we busy ourselves with goals, achievements, and relationships in an attempt to quell the rising swell of self-doubt. Fearing that we will never find the beauty we desire, or meet the expectations of those we admire, we search for the balm that will take away the sting of self-hatred.

For many years, I believed I was alone in my struggle to love myself and see myself as beautiful. Other women seemed self-assured. I had shared many secrets with friends, but not the overwhelming sense of inadequacy I felt. We talked about our love for God and our families, but we didn't share our fear that we could not learn to love ourselves.

Over the years, I have listened more closely to the voices of other women, and I have learned that I do not struggle alone.

Few people knew the deep dissatisfaction I felt toward myself when I was growing up. I always appeared to be a self-assured young woman. I had learned to bury my feelings of dislike under a mound of activities and accomplishments. I couldn't comprehend my inherent value, so I created value in a long list of club activities and academic achievements. When the voices told me I'd never be beautiful, I answered their litany of accusations with my own litany of accomplishments.

High achievements defined who I was, and failure was something I could not afford to risk. Because I could not separate what I did from who I was, to fail at what I did was to fail at who I was. I seldom attempted anything without the assurance of some measure of success. Like most people, I feared the criticism of others, but I was my own worst critic. I was afraid the opinions of others would confirm what I believed about myself.

After graduating from high school, I left home to enter college. Despite my desire to leave behind the familiar but unfriendly voices, they traveled with me.

College was much different from high school. In high school, I had received feedback on each homework assignment, quiz, test, and paper. In college, homework assignments involved large quantities of reading. Quizzes were almost nonexistent; tests and papers were assigned over the course of a whole semester and sometimes were not returned. The first month, I struggled to find my bearings. I knew that my grades had been important to me, but not until I no longer had them to use as a measurement did I realize how much they meant. I hadn't realized that I had made my grades and accomplishments the sum of who I was. Instead of paying attention to this truth when confronted with it, I tried even harder to silence it.

Activities became more important than ever. I joined clubs and vied for leadership positions on campus. But the voices were always with me. To control and suppress their tirade, I spent more time focusing on what I ate and when I exercised. While these pursuits were not wrong, my motivation was. I was unhappy with who I was, and I was attempting to find my worth in things other than God. My actions were motivated by the desire to please others rather than God.

The harder we try to silence the voices of society by finding meaning in transitory things, the louder the voices within us cry out that we have no value. I knew I was supposed to find my value in God, and even in the midst of my internal struggles, I knew God to be faithful. However, I was always left to wrestle with the abiding tension between my desire to know more of God and my desire for the approval of others.

More important, I had difficulty transferring what God thought about me to what I thought about me. I clung to the words of the prophet Jeremiah, "For I know the thoughts that I think toward you, says the LORD, thoughts of peace and not of evil, to give you a future and a hope. Then you will call upon Me and go and pray to Me, and I will listen to you. And you will seek Me and find Me, when you search for Me with all your heart" (29:11–13).

I wanted God's will for my life; I just didn't understand that God's plan for me involved accepting myself as He had made me and giving up my search for peace outside myself. When I achieved confidence in my appearance, the assurance of success, and the approval of others, I thought that then I would know God's will for my life.

When the activities left me still longing, I convinced myself that when I found my soul mate—the one with whom God would have me spend my future—I would find the longed-for peace and self-love. Having someone love and pursue me would prove to me that I had value. Surely then I would understand the depth of God's thoughts and feelings about me.

Every young girl longs for the day when she will find her knight in shining armor. Having regularly engaged in reading the timeless romance of *Anne of Green Gables*, I needed no encouragement to hope for the man who would be my Gilbert. Schoolgirl romanticism has its place in stirring our dreams and our hopes for the future, but taken to an extreme, this type of romanticism can be deceptive. From the schoolgirl point of view, the story ends as the woman and her knight marry and live happily ever after. But sometimes the perils of struggle follow the lovers as they ride off into the sunset. Sometimes the knight cannot rescue the maiden.

When I met Scott, the man who would one day be my husband, I found a godly man whom I loved and whose opinion I truly valued. But the deep places of my heart had holes that Scott could not fill. My insecurities were not healed when Scott asked me to marry him, nor when we walked down the aisle and said our vows.

Marriage does not dispel personal misgivings. If anything, it magnifies unresolved insecurities. Struggles inevitably come, and their arrival reveals the condition of our hearts. We can no longer hide behind doors marked "private." Marriage, as it should, makes us vulnerable, even in areas we pretend do not exist. The voices that I had effectively stifled while dating cried out even before we came home from the honeymoon.

Like many newlyweds, I assumed that being married would be like dating, only better. I didn't understand that dating is compartmentalized. I was involved in school, he was involved in ministry, and our time together was our own little world. However, in marriage we found ourselves distracted by little things. While dating, we had always been great communicators, but in marriage we realized that we had much to learn. Too often, I allowed my own assumptions to fill in the gaps I didn't understand about Scott. With each misunderstanding, the voices became louder and my insecurities became larger.

I had eagerly anticipated the day Scott and I would know each other intimately, but I didn't anticipate the nuances of miscommunication that sex can bring into a relationship. The idea that physical intercourse equals love is a difficult myth to dispel even when we know it is false. Without meaning to, I began using the physical aspects of our relationship to judge my husband's valuation of me. When he was too tired or too stressed for physical intimacy, I missed the opportunity to broaden my understanding of love. Instead, I listened to voices telling me that if I were thinner, he would want me regardless of whatever else he was feeling.

Even the way he spent his time became a measure of my self-worth. If I felt we weren't spending enough time together, I concluded I was not pretty enough. Because my insecurities blocked the true nature of the conflict, working toward a solution was impossible. My self-esteem issues rather than my Creator were controlling my relationship with my husband.

The irony of these voices is that my husband's voice never stopped telling me that I was beautiful or that he loved me. I simply wasn't hearing him. More accurately, I was choosing not to believe him. My marriage, while one of God's greatest gifts to me, didn't silence the voices because my insecurities went deeper than my relationship with my husband. They went to the core of who I was—to my relationship with Christ.

I knew with my head, but not with my heart, that my beauty and worth are found in Christ. Because I valued the beauty of this world, I believed that my value was in the beauty of this world. And because my values were based on the world's standards, I expected others to determine my worth in the same manner.

When I joined a Christian-based weight-loss program, I thought I had found the answer. I would silence the voices by finding the body I'd always wanted—and I would be pursuing God in the process. My motive, though, was wrong. I was joining the program not to become healthy but to be thin. I wasn't pursuing God so He could create a new heart in me; I was turning my weight loss over to God so He would create a new outward person for me to live in.

I had found a way to stifle the voices, but they still were not silent. When I looked in the mirror and heard *I'm so fat*, I followed the program more vigorously and fought the voices with my fat-gram tally sheet. When I looked in the mirror and heard *No one sees me as beautiful*, I replayed all the compliments I had heard from others on my weight loss. When I looked in the mirror and heard *I'll never have it together like other women*, I looked at the smaller pant-size that now fit.

But I wasn't really defeating the voices. I was feeding them. As long as I was losing weight, I could accept myself. My value still came down to my external appearance. Only now I had made losing weight a spiritual discipline. I even began to equate being thin with being spiritual.

Thirteen weeks into the program, I had lost twenty-two pounds. I had never felt so good about myself. I hadn't been so thin since hitting puberty. I not only felt in control of my weight, I felt in control of my spirituality. Pursuing God had become much more formulaic. Eating fried chicken was sinful while eating raw vegetables was godly. Likewise, the more I exercised, the more spiritual I felt. I believed that because I had been unhappy with myself, God had been unhappy with me. I believed that my pain and insecurity were consequences of not being the thin person God wanted me to be. Now that I was thin, I could begin to please God. But my contentment hung by a tenuous thread.

Once I met my weight goal, I began the maintenance segment of the program. Because I had become accustomed to holding rigid boundaries on my eating, I was uncertain how to return certain foods into my diet. My worst fear was that I would gain back the weight I had worked so hard to lose. When I did begin to gain weight, my self-esteem wasn't the only part of me that took a hit. I believed that I had not only failed the program and myself but also God.

I had asked God to change the way I looked, to help me

diet, to help me exercise every day, to help me find the right clothes, to make me anyone but me. But in all my asking for solutions to my insecurities, I had never asked Him to change my heart. Until one Sunday afternoon.

Arriving home from church, I walked to the bedroom and curled up on the bed, dress clothes and all. I had reached the bottom. Feeling broken and emotionally spent, I began to cry. I begged God to change me. Saying the words aloud for the first time, I told God I hated my body and I hated myself. But I did not want to continue hating myself, and I did not want to continue chasing the shadowy image of beauty the world had offered me. On that day, I stopped asking God to make me thin and beautiful. Instead, I asked God to teach me to understand the beauty He sees in me. Those simple words began a journey—a journey to understand priceless beauty from the heart of One who paid the price with His life.

My struggle with the voices within has taught me that I must find my value in the One who gives me value. Surrounding myself with achievements and accomplishments cannot convince me of my value, seeking love from others cannot convince me of my value, and changing the way I look cannot convince me of my value.

The voices within thrive upon weakness. But a deeper message is waiting to be heard: *We were made for something more.* Contrary to what the voices tell us, we cannot become the more that we feel lacking. God is to be our strength, and His strength is made perfect in our weakness (2 Corinthians 12:9).

In our battle against the voices within and without, we must recognize four important truths.

First, we must allow the words that we hear from others to be filtered through Scripture, which indicates the thoughts on which we are to dwell:

> Finally, brethren, whatever things are true, whatever things are noble, whatever things are just, whatever things are pure, whatever things are lovely, whatever things are of good report, if there is any virtue and if there is anything praiseworthy— meditate on these things. (Philippians 4:8)

Constructive criticism has its place, but accusations of failure and inadequacy do not. When we hear what others say about us and about themselves, we must determine whether our rehearsal of those comments will strengthen or undermine our understanding of who we are in Christ. Listening is a choice; it is actively attending to information. We hear words of failure in our minds because we actively choose to give them an audience.

Second, we must change the way we speak about ourselves. Maybe we're fishing for compliments, maybe we really believe what we say, or maybe we think that if we hurt ourselves first, then others' words won't hurt as much. Or perhaps the negative comments are a poor attempt at humility. We think that saying negative things about ourselves will keep us from becoming prideful and thus make us spiritual.

Whatever the reason, the result is the same. When we deride ourselves, we curse God's creation. We essentially tell God, "I know You called it good, but I don't believe it's good enough." How can we claim to praise and worship God and, with the same mouth, curse His creation? Scripture says, "Let the words of my mouth and the meditation of my heart be acceptable in Your sight, O LORD, my strength and my Redeemer" (Psalm 19:14) and Jesus taught, "out of the abundance of the heart [the] mouth speaks" (Luke 6:45). Words of denigration reveal a heart problem. Our heart is listening to the life-taker and not the Life-Giver.

Third, we must learn to identify the words spoken by the one who seeks to destroy our souls. Satan is a liar. We know that he comes only "to steal, and to kill, and to destroy" (John 10:10). Deception is at the core of his being, and thus everything he speaks is void of truth. We can identify his words when we hear them—he speaks words of rejection, hatred, failure, and discontent.

"I'll never measure up."

"I can never be beautiful."

"I am the sum of all my failures."

"If I were thinner, I'd be happier."

"If I were prettier, people would love me."

"I'm not good at anything."

"I'm so ugly."

"I need to change the way I look."

"If I had new clothes, I'd be satisfied with the way I look."

"I'm so fat."

All lies. Words of death, not life. If he can convince us that we're worthless, he can immobilize us and keep us from fulfilling God's plan for our lives. Out of fear of rejection, we won't reach out to others. We'll wallow in self-hatred. Out of fear of failure, we won't follow our dreams. We'll drown in discontent.

The clamor of voices rings in our heads while we bravely paste smiles on our faces. We quietly tell ourselves that we must live with the voices and pretend to have the peace and self-assurance that we long for but which slip through our fingers with every self-deprecating word. And then the voices become more vicious.

"If God really cared, He wouldn't have made you look this way."

"If you can't believe God loves you just the way you are, His love must not be true."

"If you were really spiritual, you wouldn't struggle to love yourself."

Lies. All lies. When we call them what they are, they lose their power and the truth becomes clearer. Beauty does exist, and God waits for us like a patient lover.

Finally, we must hear what God has to say about us.

> *Before the beginning of time, I knew you. I knew what color your eyes would be, and I could hear the sound of your laughter. Like a proud father who carries a picture of his daughter, I carried the image of you in My eyes, for you were created in My image Before the beginning of time, I chose you. I spoke your name into the heavens, and I smiled as its melody resounded off the walls of My heart.*
>
> *You are Mine. My love for you extends farther than the stars in the sky and deeper than any ocean. You are My pearl of great price, the one for whom I gave everything. I cradle you in the palm of My hand. I love you even in the face of your failure. Nothing you say or do*

*can cause Me to stop loving you. I am relentless in My
pursuit of you. Run from Me—I will love you. Spurn
Me—I will love you. Reject yourself—I will love you. You
see, My love for you was slain before the foundations of
the world and I have never regretted the sacrifice I made
for you at Calvary.*

*When I see every part of who you are, I marvel at the
work of My hands, for I whispered words of longing and
desire and you came into existence. You are beautiful,
and I take pleasure in you—heart, mind, and body. You
are My desire. When you turn your head in shame and
despise what I have made, still I reach for you with gentle
passion. You are My beloved and I am yours.* (Author's
adaptation from 1 John 3:2; Isaiah 43:1; Matthew
13:46; Ephesians 1:4; Revelation 13:8; Psalm 194:4;
Song of Solomon 7:10; 6:3).

God longs for us to know His beauty, but we must
choose how to respond to the voices we hear.

The voices from without and within skew reality.
Hearing God's voice above the destructive invective is an
ongoing struggle. We may never silence the voices, but we
can choose whether or not the voices define who we are.
God stands waiting to lead us on a journey to know true
beauty, a journey that begins by listening carefully to His
heart and gazing into the mirror of His Word.

LOOKING IN THE MIRROR
Personal Reflection

1. Filter through Scripture the words you hear from others.

Reflect on the "voices without" that influence the way you view yourself. You may want to refer back to the personal application section of chapter two. Consider these voices in light of what God's Word says.

As you go through your day, be mindful of those voices that play over in your mind. When you hear something that does not line up with Philippians 4:8, stop and ask the Lord to help you focus on words that please Him and reflect His perceptions of truth and beauty.

2. Change the way you speak about yourself.

Evaluate your own speech. What negative things do you say about yourself? Why?

Take this issue before the Lord in prayer.

3. Learn to identify the words spoken by the one who seeks to destroy your soul.

Write down some of the lies that Satan levels against you. When these lies begin to form in your mind, speak the truth and call them lies. Find a Scripture verse to counter each lie; cross out the lie and write the biblical truth next to it.

4. Hear what God says about you.

Having read what God knows and believes about you, write a response to Him. Be honest in your response.

MIRROR, MIRROR

I CANNOT remember the exact day the mirror became my prison, but I knew I was being held against my will when I realized I was seeking affirmation from an object that could only reflect what I chose to see. Certainly there were some days when I walked away from my morning mirror routine thinking, "Not too bad." But more often were the "if only" days. "If only my hair were longer." "If only my hair were shorter." "If only I were taller." "If only my eyes were brown." And the ever present "If only I were thinner."

At other times, the mirror is my courtroom where a jury of one, biased by whimsy and mood, delivers a verdict of my worth.

Mirrors are a part of every woman's life. Nicole Johnson poignantly described the anxiety women feel when they see their own bodies:

The terror creeps up my spine before I even get out of bed. I know what lies ahead today. I stay completely still and let the safety of the covers envelop me. Maybe if I ignore it, it will go away. The hard work that will fill my day already drains every ounce of energy in my body. The dread of all the walking, the endless barrage of searching, the tears.

I have to buy a swimsuit today.

What is it about that one purchase that makes my knees weak and my self-esteem plummet? Maybe it's thinking about looking at my body under lights that pick up things the Hubble telescope would miss. Maybe it's the fact that the top of my legs look like the surface of the moon. Perhaps it's the futility of trying to make a stretchy piece of fabric the size of a pot holder cover the square mile of my rear end. But somehow this one activity moves me from a self-confident, mature woman to feeling like I'm back in junior high.[1]

The more we gaze in the mirror of worldly images, the more vulnerable we feel. To wage war against unflattering images painted by fluorescent lighting in department store dressing room mirrors, I adjust my view of my vulnerable body with varied poses and slanted eyes.

Especially troubling are unexpected mirror moments. While strolling through the mall with an iced mocha topped with mounds of whipped cream—suddenly, a mirror. On these occasions I ask myself, "Is that really me?" That question begins an avalanche of self-assessment: do my hips really stick out that far; do my breasts really hang that low; and why don't I feel as short as I look?

The irony of mirrors is their drawing power. I am enticed by the possibility that the next mirror I look into will show me what I want to see. Maybe then I will be content. But therein also lies the problem. I expect to find contentment when *I like what I see*. How can I like what I see when I gaze with worldly eyes upon an image that was not created by the world?

Equally troubling is my lack of recognition when I unexpectedly see myself in the mirror. How can I not recognize a face that I see every day while brushing my teeth? Perhaps I do not recognize the face I see because my "powers of adjustment" have a commanding influence over my self-perception and my memory.

Jay Gatsby, the protagonist in F. Scott Fitzgerald's novel *The Great Gatsby*, recreates himself and his surroundings to please his beloved Daisy. When he is reunited with her after many years, he views his staged world through her eyes and finds that "It is invariably saddening to look through new eyes at things upon which you have expended your own powers of adjustment."[2]

He surrenders his being to the illusion of the American dream and society's expectations. Eventually, he can no longer distinguish the real Gatsby from the created Gatsby. What Gatsby never grasps is the truth that his illusions can never measure up to Daisy's or society's expectations because they require a denial of who he truly is. In the end, his broken dreams lead him to both spiritual and physical death.

Like Gatsby, I try to recreate myself into a well-staged self, or I deny those parts of myself that do not fit the world's definition of beauty. Both acts leave me wondering who I am and longing to be known. Sadly, my preoccupation with the image of the world rather than the image of Christ leaves me broken, like Gatsby, and unable to recognize the woman God has created me to be.

Many times I have stepped in front of the mirror and hoped to discover my true self, as if the glass had the power to reveal who I am. There is only one place, though, where I can find my true reflection. The eyes of my Creator, my Father God, reflect the answers to my deepest longings for self-worth, my deepest desires to be known.

As Christian women, we must uphold the truth that Scripture is the mirror of beauty through which we view ourselves. Because we live in a culture driven by visual images, we may find ourselves looking for visual pictures of physical beauty in Scripture to serve as a scale for our own self-measurement. How tall was Queen Esther? How much did Ruth weigh? How long did it take Mary to return to her pre-pregnancy weight? What color were Rachel's eyes?

In the beginning we were created in the image of God (Genesis 1:27), and Scripture even defines some individuals as being physically beautiful. Rachel was "beautiful of form and appearance" (Genesis 29:17). David was described as "ruddy, with bright eyes, and good-looking" (1 Samuel 16:12) and Abigail as "a woman of good understanding and beautiful appearance" (1 Samuel 25:3). Likewise, Bathsheba "was very beautiful to behold" (2 Samuel 11:2) and Absalom was praised for his looks (2 Samuel 14:25). In the story of

Esther, the author mentions the beauty of both Vashti and Esther (Esther 1:11; 2:7). And finally, Solomon says of his beloved, "O my love, you are as beautiful as Tirzah, lovely as Jerusalem" (Song of Solomon 6:4).

However, these passages fail to define beauty. We are told nothing about hairstyles, hip size, breast size, weight, or height.

Too often, we equate God's standard of beauty with the world's. Many are the women of character, integrity, and honor of whom Scripture says little as to the beauty of their physical appearances: Jael, Deborah, Ruth, Mary, Anna, to name a few. God's definition of beauty comes to us differently than we might expect.

To understand true beauty, I must understand to Whom I belong. The world did not create me and does not know me. God did and does. My existence came of the will of God, the all-knowing, all-powerful Creator who sees the works of His hands and calls them "good." The apostle John says, "But as many as received Him, to them He gave the right to become children of God, to those who believe in His name: who were born, not of blood, nor of the will of the flesh, nor of the will of man, but of God" (John 1:12–13). I was created in a magnificent outpouring of God's love, and I am chosen.

What then is God's definition of beauty?

We find the answer in a passage pivotal to Christianity but seldom considered when defining beauty: "For God so loved the world that He gave His only begotten Son, that whoever believes in Him should not perish but have everlasting life" (John 3:16).

Perhaps you wonder how this Scripture defines beauty.

The most beautiful act between God and man was God's offering of His own Son to be the sacrifice for our sin. God's beauty is pure and undefiled. God's beauty is eternal and gives life. God's beauty requires ultimate vulnerability, a nakedness of the soul before God. God's beauty is true because it is the truth. Salvation is all these things: "For the LORD takes pleasure in His people; He will beautify the humble with salvation" (Psalm 149:4). Salvation is true beauty, God's definition of beauty. Because I have been bought with that which is eternal, I cannot find my understanding of beauty in that which is temporal.

When I base my value on the standards of the world, my love for myself is conditional. I promise to love myself *if* I lose weight, *if* I like the way I look, *if* I earn the approval of others, *if* I succeed in my endeavors. But God's love for me is unconditional. He will never love me any more or any less than He does at this moment in time.

Consider the irony that we are to find our beauty in One who is described as having "no form or comeliness; . . . no beauty that we should desire Him" (Isaiah 53:2). Because of the world's superficial understanding of beauty, those who are worldly cannot see the true beauty of Christ; thus they perceive Him as having "no form or comeliness." However, because God is the One from whom true beauty emanates, Christ is beauty incarnate, not according to the world's definition but God's.

Thus, a woman's beauty must be found in and defined by things that are eternal, life-giving, and true. We must desire things that draw us to Christ and bring us to fullness of life in Him. He is our salvation; so too He is our beauty. The only way we will ever know true, pure physical beauty is to seek a life of true, pure spiritual beauty.

The book of Ruth never mentions Ruth's physical appearance. But whenever I read her story, I perceive her as beautiful because her choices exhibit true beauty and true character. She pursued the eternal in her decision to serve the one, true God. She then lived out this grace and brought life to those around her, specifically to Naomi, her mother-in-law, and to Boaz, her future husband. Finally, she sought things that were pure and true, as evidenced by the words Boaz said to her, "[A]ll the people of my town know that you are a virtuous woman" (Ruth 3:11b).

By the world's standards, Ruth may have been homely or beautiful; we don't know. However, the question of her physical attractiveness is irrelevant in light of her determination to pursue God. The beauty of her character surpassed her physical appearance and became the true beauty by which her life was marked.

The story of Ruth exemplifies that a woman of God becomes beautiful when she worships the One who is beauty. The Psalms resonate with the relationship between the beauty of the Lord and worship: "One thing I have desired of the LORD, that will I seek: that I may dwell in the house of the LORD all the days of my life, to behold the beauty of the LORD, and to inquire [NASB *meditate*] in His temple" (Psalm 27:4).

When we abandon ourselves to a passionate life of worship, we see God's beauty and find our own—in Him. When we lose ourselves in a life of worship to an omnipotent God, we find the purpose for which we were created. Suddenly, the things of this world, including its standard of beauty, become meaningless. The psalmist wrote, "Honor and majesty are before Him; strength and beauty are in His sanctuary. . . . Oh, worship the LORD in the beauty of holiness!" (Psalm 96:6, 9a). In worship, false pretenses and artificial longings—our own and those of others—fall away before a holy, awesome God. When I stand and consider the majesty of His name and the works of His hands, my weight, my height, my cup size, and my hairstyle cease to matter.

Immersing ourselves in worship does not finish the definition of beauty; it merely begins the discussion. Perhaps you've heard the saying, "Pretty is as pretty does." The beauty of God that we discover in worship must emanate from our lives. Our lives will radiate beauty when we "let the beauty of the LORD our God be upon us, and establish the work of our hands for us; yes, establish the work of our hands" (Psalm 90:17). Taking on the nature of Christ, our physical appearance becomes a vessel for the beauty of Christ to shine through.

Consider again the story of Ruth. Because she devoted herself to worship, her life produced excellence and beauty, and she became a part of the lineage of the One who is beauty for all (Matthew 1:5). True beauty is a life lived for Christ.

People today spend millions, perhaps billions, of dollars seeking to restore the beauty of their youth. God seeks to restore our beauty, but not through tummy tucks, face lifts, miracle creams, or trendy hairstyles. He longs to restore our beauty from deep within.

Understanding the harlotry of worldly beauty, the prophet Hosea provided a picture of true beauty. In speaking of the restoration of Israel, he wrote, "His branches shall spread; His beauty shall be like an olive tree, and his fragrance like Lebanon" (Hosea 14:6). Old Testament scholar Marvin Wilson explains this imagery in his book *Our Father Abraham*:

> To those from the Occident (West), the olive tree, with its gnarled trunk and soft, gray-green leaves, does not appear to be an especially beautiful tree. But to those from the Orient (East), the olive tree has an artistic appearance that has been admired for ages. . . . Olive trees were famous for their longevity. . . . The roots of the olive tree (cf. Rom. 11:18) are remarkably sturdy, thriving in the rocky soil and the hot, dry climate of the land. . . . [O]live trees were prized for their fruitfulness. . . . [And the] olive branch has long symbolized peace (cf. Gen. 8:11).[3]

Women inundated by images of the world's beauty can find true beauty only by hearing and applying God's message of beauty. Planted deeply in the soil of worship, we find restored beauty in knowing that we are uniquely created by an artistic God, that He modeled ultimate beauty for us in the gift of Christ's sacrifice, that we are created for things which are eternal, and that we can bring forth the fruit of Christ because salvation in Him produces a beautiful life.

Worship teaches me what it means to possess true beauty and satisfies my deep longings to be known. The apostle Paul wrote, "But if anyone loves God, this one is known by Him" (1 Corinthians 8:3). The "Is that really me?" questions of my heart are answered in knowing that the One who willed me into existence and who knows me also loves me.

However, my knowledge of myself and of God will be veiled on earth, as Paul recognized when he wrote, "For now we see in a mirror, dimly, but then face to face. Now I know in part, but then I shall know just as I also am known" (1 Corinthians 13:12).

But my limitations do not limit an infinite God. I am already "fully known" by the One who knows and sees all. This truth reconciles the tension between my deepest longings to be known and my understanding that my own knowledge will be limited this side of heaven. Reaching out in faith, I must rest in the knowledge that God intimately knows me, and that *His* knowing creates a divine destiny for my life.

Mirror, mirror on the wall, I know who's fairest of all. His name is Jesus, and because of Him I cannot define beauty as this world does. The physical and spiritual are intricately linked, and I must live a life governed by the Spirit. Therefore, the models of beauty that I seek to emulate must be women of worship whose lives are governed by the Spirit of God and exhibit the fruit of Christ. As I walk past my reflection in mirrors and store windows, I must choose to view myself through either the mirror of God's Word or the mirror of this world. The choice I make is the difference between life and death. It is the difference between creating an idol and being the temple.

LOOKING IN THE MIRROR
Personal Reflection

We often segment ourselves into aspects we like about ourselves and those we don't. For example, a woman might say that she likes her eyes but hates her legs. Do you see yourself in terms of parts?

Did God create parts of us in His image or all of us in His image?

Did Jesus die to redeem parts of who we are or all of our being—body, mind, and spirit?

Does your definition of beauty reflect God's idea of wholistic redemption? Why or why not?

Worship is a life lived in the presence of God. Ask the Lord to teach you (or continue to teach you) what it means to live before Him moment by moment.

How does worship bring freedom from the world's standard of beauty?

Keeping in mind that Zion is a place of praise, read Psalm 50:2. Explain how this Scripture applies to a proper understanding of beauty.

Read James 1:23–25. What does this Scripture teach about the Word as a mirror for our lives? In other words, if we are a reflection of the image of God, what will we do?

DOLS AND TEMPLES

SHE tries to hide the doubts and fears that weigh her down, but her actions speak volumes.

She, too, hears the voices. To place sacrifices at the feet of the idols, she destroys her temple. There are no golden calves or statues of Baal hidden in her home, but look in the secrets of her heart, the hidden places of her insecurities, and her idols abound. Idols and temples are not all made of brick, stone, or gold.

Everyday actions, so routine they become a part of who we are. We cannot recognize the idolatry in our own behavior, much less that we are the sacrifice.

IDOL WORSHIP. Different women, different rituals. The same desire. Acceptance. Acceptance from others and from self. The woman who spins endlessly in the cycle of fad dieting in search of the perfect figure. The woman who needs expensive jewelry to feel priceless. The woman who weighs herself before and after going to the bathroom in hopes that the numbers will change. The woman who believes she is only as good as she looks. The woman who obsesses over everything she eats, calculating the calories and fat with each bite. The woman who changes her hair color to match her mood as she searches for the look that makes her feel comfortable with herself. The woman who takes diet pills to lose "just a few more pounds." The woman who cannot go out in public without makeup because she feels too vulnerable. The woman who cannot eat at public gatherings out of fear that others will judge what she eats. The woman who cannot miss a workout at the gym and who berates herself if she shortens her time on the treadmill. The woman who binges and purges, desperately seeking to control not only her weight but also her life. Different women, different rituals. The same bondage.

Unhappy. Powerless. Enslaved. Our idols are varied, but they leave us with similar feelings. The truth of our idolatry is poignant: we care more about what others think of us than what God thinks of us.

Although we do not bow down or pray to gods of gold and stone, we bow to the image of this world when we continually measure ourselves by the world's standards of success and beauty. Not only are we unable to recognize our beauty in Christ, we often distort what He has made in our desperate attempt to recast ourselves in the world's image. We sell our true beauty for handfuls of dirt when we allow external features to determine our worth. Convincing ourselves that the world knows more about assessing beauty than does the Creator of beauty, we trade the eternal for the temporal, purity for sensuality, integrity for acceptance.

Israel, too, traded her spiritual beauty for the idolatrous beauty of the world. Speaking against the Israelites' desecration of God's temple, the prophet Ezekiel declared, "As for the beauty of his ornaments, He set it in majesty; but they made from it the images of their abominations" (Ezekiel 7:20a). Because of spiritual adultery, Israel suffered great destruction and was unable to find peace (Ezekiel 7:25).

While we are not being held by iron chains, and our homes are not being razed by marauding armies, our idolatry brings us into bondage nonetheless. We become bound to the standards of the world rather than to the standards of the cross.

Meanwhile, to appear spiritual, we loudly proclaim from our prisons that eternal things matter more than anything temporal. But what do our lives say? Do we focus more on what we feed our bodies or on what we feed our souls? Do we spend more time sculpting our bodies than shaping our devotional life? Do we more readily seek comfort from food or from the Holy Spirit? Do we spend more time perfecting our physical appearance or preparing our heart? Do we spend more money investing in self-improvement or in the work of God's kingdom? Are we more drawn to those who reflect the world's image of beauty and success or to those who radiate the image of God?

Scripture speaks clearly about the issue of a divided heart. We cannot seek the glory of the world and the glory of God.

Eventually we will embody either God's definition of beauty or the world's. When we focus on finding our meaning and value in the world, we miss seeing God. Jesus asked, "How can you believe, who receive honor from one another, and do not seek the honor that comes from the only God?" (John 5:44). Whose honor do we seek? Whose opinion really matters? Whose definition of beauty will we embody?

We may effectively hide our idolatries from those around us, but the God whose eyes have seen our unformed substance (Psalm 139:16a) is the same God who knows the things we worship in the deepest places of our hearts. He sees the core of who we are, and He knows that while we glorify Him with our lips, we continue our pursuit of worldly beauty. Sadly, we often fail to recognize the duality within our own hearts. We awaken from our self-deluded state to find ourselves trapped in an adulterous relationship with the world. We awaken to find that we have abandoned the Lover of our Souls in exchange for emptiness.

In his novel *The Scarlet Letter*, Nathaniel Hawthorne details the destruction of a divided heart in the character of the Reverend Dimmesdale. Having been involved in an adulterous relationship with a married parishioner and being too cowardly to confess, Dimmesdale undergoes both physical and spiritual deterioration as he struggles to continue his public ministry while hiding his sin. Cautioning against the resulting confusion of living with a divided heart, Hawthorne says of Dimmesdale, "No man for any considerable period, can wear one face to himself, another to the multitude, without finally getting bewildered as to which may be the true."[1]

The greatest consequence of living with a divided heart is the eventual inability to know which love will bring life and which will bring death.

Although Dimmesdale attempts to continue the life of a blameless shepherd to his flock, he learns the painful lesson that the outer and inner man are intricately linked. His physical act of adultery affects his spiritual well-being, and in turn, his spiritual sickness begins to play out in the decay of his body. While Dimmesdale's adultery was physical in nature, his sin demonstrates that adultery begins in the heart when we allow any desire to surpass our desire for God.

When we focus more on changing our bodies than on changing our hearts, we have chosen the world. Theologian Abraham Wright wrote,

> Many are shamed to be seen as God made them; few are ashamed to be seen what the devil hath made them. Many are troubled at small defects in the outward man; few are troubled at the greatest deformities of the inward man; many buy artificial beauty to supply the natural; few spiritual, to supply the defects of the supernatural beauty of the soul.[2]

Wright lived in the seventeenth century. If society then was obsessed with external beauty, how much more so today? Many of us are guilty of being more concerned with what others see than what God sees.

DESTRUCTION OF THE TEMPLE. With her head tucked down and her arms at her side, she approaches the building.

She is well acquainted with the simple structure. She has entered it every day for twenty-nine years. The cross at the apex of the roof quietly reaches toward her. Peace. The strong, pierced hands sculpted into the door beckon her to enter. Safety. The cup and the bread on the table gently whisper her name. Intimacy. Her head still lowered, she crosses the threshold. Sanctuary.

As she enters the building, she slowly lifts her head and gazes around her. She reaches into her pocket and grasps one of the heavy rocks she carries. Gripping it, she approaches the altar with her hand outstretched. She can feel its jagged edges pressing painfully into her skin. When she reaches her destination, she turns. With her back to the altar, she looks out the nearest window. The incoming sunlight dances off the tear that glides down her cheek.

I hate you. Her piercing shriek echoes off the wall, and the sound of shattering glass is heard as she hurls the rock through the window. *You are a disappointment.* Another rock leaves her hand and shatters another window. *You will never measure up.* The cup and the bread tumble to the floor with the fury of her pain. Rock after rock. The words resonate off the walls until nothing else can be heard. Rock after rock. Brokenness lies around her. Brokenness lies within her. Gone is the peace. Gone is the safety. Gone is the intimacy. Slumped on her knees, her head tucked down, her hands now empty, she grieves for what she has lost. Sanctuary.

Hearing the buzz of her alarm, she reluctantly climbs from her bed and heads toward the bathroom. Leaning over the sink, she gently splashes cold water on her face. As she lifts her head, she gazes into the mirror. *Ugh, I look terrible this morning.* She moves to her closet and looks through her clothes. Nothing seems to satisfy her as she grabs one item, only to replace it with another. *Nothing looks good on me anymore.* Finally, she decides on an outfit. After dressing, she returns to the mirror to finish her morning routine. *I am so fat.* Word after word, rock after rock. Her soul hears the breaking glass, and the words resonate off the walls until nothing else can be heard.

Looking in the mirror, she wonders why she feels broken even before her day has begun.

In Christian circles, we speak freely about the importance of guarding the temple of our bodies in regard to what we watch, hear, eat, and do. Rarely, however, do we draw a connection between the words we say about ourselves and the fact that we are speaking about God's temple. We would never consider vandalizing our local place of worship, but we don't think twice about damaging ourselves with self-deprecating thoughts and words. The impact is the same.

Believing we will find the very things that we cannot find in this world, we reverently enter the temple of the Most High God. We teach our children not to run in the sanctuary and to respect the building where we gather on Sundays. While it is important to demonstrate respect toward the church structure, Scripture is clear that the Spirit of God does not dwell in buildings made of brick and stone but in the flesh and blood created in His image. Paul wrote, "Do you not know that you are the temple of God and that the Spirit of God dwells in you?" (1 Corinthians 3:16). Our being the temple is a beautiful concept. As we enter into communion with God, He takes residence within us. The very essence of our spiritual being, which is dead before He enters us, becomes more alive than the physical bodies in which we reside. Seeking peace, safety, and intimacy, we find within ourselves our reason for living because Christ lives in us. However, we cannot find peace, safety, or intimacy in a heart that hurls accusations of inadequacy and failure against itself. And where there is no peace, safety, or intimacy, there is no sanctuary.

Just as we cannot imagine vandalizing a sanctuary of brick and stone, we cannot imagine such a crime going unpunished. At the very least, we would expect the guilty individual to accept responsibility. Any denial of wrongdoing or shrugging off the seriousness of the offense would grate against our sense of justice. Most of all, we would expect him to understand that it was not simply an architectural structure he had violated. His act of vandalism violated the sense of peace, safety, and intimacy associated with worship. His reckless act destroyed our sanctuary.

Like one who destroys the sanctuary human hands build, we must accept responsibility when we destroy the temple God creates. We cannot go on thinking that the words we level against ourselves don't matter. We know that words matter, or we wouldn't ask of the Lord, "Let the words of my mouth and the meditation of my heart be acceptable in Your sight" (Psalm 19:14).

Thoughts and words that disparage us physically, mentally, or spiritually are the rocks that destroy the temple of God. God declares that such an act of vandalism will not go unpunished. Even in His infinite mercy and grace, God's nature demands justice. Paul wrote, "If anyone defiles the temple of God, God will destroy him. For the temple of God is holy, which temple you are" (1 Corinthians 3:17). Our inability to understand our own inherent true beauty destroys the very beauty that results from our being the temple of God. Gone is the peace, the safety, the intimacy. Gone is the sanctuary. If we do not value the temple, we cease to be the temple.

THE APPROPRIATE SACRIFICE. Before you begin to think that I believe women should not wear makeup and jewelry and should dress in burlap sacks, let me qualify my message.

A carving of stone or gold is not an idol in and of itself. The heart of the worshiper is what makes an object an idol. Jewelry, makeup, and clothing do not have the power to be idols in and of themselves. The motive of my heart (what I desire from those things) determines whether or not they are idols. If I need jewelry, makeup, or fashionable clothing to feel valuable, I have transformed those objects into idols because I expect from them what I can receive only from the One I claim to worship.

Chasing the elusive promise of physical beauty is no less destructive than eschewing such beauty to the point of martyrdom. Women need not put aside jewelry and makeup to be spiritual. On the contrary, labeling all makeup and jewelry as sinful is the opposite side of the same counterfeit coin that focuses attention on the physical rather than the spiritual. It's just another way of being more concerned with external appearance than internal character. Anything that regards physical qualities rather than spiritual fruit as a gauge of spirituality is misguided and destructive.

Nor am I advocating that we eat or live without regard to our physical nature. God created us as both spiritual and physical beings. I cannot ignore that what I eat, and how much, affects my body; neither can I ignore that my body was created for movement; thus activity is vital to my well-being. I am simply saying that I cannot allow food and exercise to determine my value. I must seek God's wisdom to hold all these things in balance.

After all, my body is the temple.

Consequently, my body does not belong to me. In the same way that God expects me to use the talents He has given me in service to Him, so also He expects me to give my body to Him.

> Or do you not know that your body is the temple of
> the Holy Spirit, who is in you, whom you have
> from God, and you are not your own? For you were
> bought at a price; therefore glorify God in your
> body and in your spirit, which are God's.
> (1 Corinthians 6:19–20)

When I long for the world's beauty, I must remember the price that was paid for me, for my body. When I am tempted to denigrate my physical appearance, I must remember that my body, as well as my spirit, belongs to God.

I am a sacrifice, but not to the idolatrous beauty of this world. Paul admonished us to present our "bodies a living sacrifice, holy, acceptable to God, which is [our] reasonable service" (Romans 12:1). The New American Standard Bible's translation of the latter part of this passage says that presenting our bodies as a sacrifice is our "spiritual service of worship." Thus, my body is not only the place where the living God resides; it is also a tool to be used for the glory of God, a means of worshiping Him. Because my body is a sacrifice to God, all things in my life are subject to God's authority—the way I dress, eat, and live. But God doesn't require that we become legalistic; He's more interested in our motives. Jesus came to bring us abundant, beautiful life. He came to bring us freedom.

We have a choice. Freedom or bondage. We need not remain bound to the world's image of beauty. Nor must we remain broken by the destructive forces of culture:

> For those who live according to the flesh set their minds on the things of the flesh, but those who live according to the Spirit, the things of the Spirit. For to be carnally minded is death, but to be spiritually minded is life and peace. (Romans 8:5–6)

When we choose life, we choose transformation.

LOOKING IN THE MIRROR
Personal Application

"But now that you have come to know God, or rather to be known by God, how is it that you turn back again to the weak and worthless elemental things, to which you desire to be enslaved all over again?" (Galatians 4:9 NASB). The apostle Paul wrote these words to describe the freedom we have in Christ. Although Paul was writing against the works-based faith of the Judaizers, this passage helps us understand that our pursuit of the world's beauty places us in bondage, while our pursuit of God's beauty brings us freedom.

Why is the world's standard of beauty "weak and worthless"?

In what ways are you still "desir[ing] to be enslaved all over again" to the world's beauty?

Take a moment to examine your heart. Think about those places in your life where you still struggle with insecurities about your worth. Identify some of these areas of struggles.

In what ways do these struggles connect to your concern with what others think of you?

An idol is something other than God that we rely on, or something other than God from which we derive our identity. Being concerned with others' opinions of us can be helpful in our lives as it can motivate us to make good choices. However, we often focus too much on impressing others. Caring what others think about us because we want them to see Christ is much different than caring what others think about us because we want them to think well of us. Has your concern for others' opinions become an idol in your life? In other words, what drives your actions more: what others think of you or what God thinks of you? Read John 5:44 as you answer this question.

What other elements of physical beauty have become idols in your life?

Read 1 Peter 1:18–19. Explain how this Scripture relates to your value as the temple of the living God.

Do your thoughts about yourself destroy the temple within you? If so, be specific as to how these thoughts tear down what God desires to build in you.

What areas of your body do you still need to offer as a sacrifice to Him?

Read Galatians 5:1. Paraphrase this Scripture as it applies to your journey to understand God's beauty.

 NEW PERSPECTIVE

ONE summer, my husband and I took a group of
teenagers to inner-city Chicago for a missions trip. As our
host drove us to our downtown housing, we could see in the
distance two very large buildings, one obviously taller than
the other. We asked him if the taller building was the Sears
Tower. To our surprise, he said the building we had
mistaken to be the Sears Tower was in fact the John
Hancock Building. A little arrogant and very ignorant, I
determined that our host either didn't get out much or was
unaware that the Sears Tower was the tallest building in
Chicago. The tower he was identifying as the John Hancock
Building was obviously much larger than the building he
claimed was the Sears Tower.

As we continued around the city, however, our
perspective changed, and our view eventually matched what

our host had asserted. The taller became the shorter, and the shorter became the tallest of all—and the difference was visually significant.

That day I learned that perspective depends on where I stand.

Earlier that same summer, my husband and I had traveled to New Jersey to visit some college friends. I had not seen any of them in at least four years. In that time I had gained thirty pounds, and I found myself wrestling with issues that I thought I had put to rest. While I was visiting one friend in particular, God led me down a new path in understanding His beauty.

We had become friends during my sophomore year in college when she served as resident assistant on my floor of the dorm. Our fathers had both been pastors in the same denomination, so we shared a kindred spirit. Now both married and pursuing our respective callings, we greeted one another with joy—and surprise. Like me, she had gained some weight over the years. No longer did I feel the pressure to look the same as I had as a college sophomore, and no longer did I worry what she would think of the changes in my body.

As we began talking about the things God had been teaching us, I learned that we both struggled to see our true beauty. While my friend and I paged through a picture album from our college days, God taught me an important lesson in perspective. Flipping through the memories, she casually commented, "Do you know what I think of when I see these pictures? I think of how much skinnier I was back then." I sat quietly for a moment as I reflected on her words.

Then I responded, "I, too, think of how much skinnier I was in these pictures. But I also remember how fat I *thought* I was when these pictures were taken. Even then I wasn't satisfied with who I was or how I looked."

The pictures reminded me of the times I have looked for someone with my exact body size and shape so that I could objectively evaluate how I looked. But whenever I try to evaluate my beauty, I lose all objectivity and perspective, for I see myself through worldly eyes, and I am dissatisfied with whatever I see. I have never been thin enough, pretty enough, or talented enough. I am forever falling short of the mark. But my greatest failure is not missing the mark of the world. My greatest failure is my inability to see that God's beauty stands far above the beauty of the world—and the difference between the two is visually significant.

Just as I had to have the proper perspective to see which building was the tallest in downtown Chicago, so too I need the proper perspective to see which beauty is true—the world's or God's.

Things that are true reveal beauty, and things that are beautiful reveal truth. Eighteenth-century English poet John Keats wrote, "Truth is beauty; beauty truth. That is all ye know and all ye need to know."[1] So if I want to know beauty, I need to know Truth. If I want to live in beauty, I must live in Truth.

Proper perspective occurs when we see as God sees. Therefore, to have a true and right perspective on beauty, I must find my identity in the One who sees as God sees. In other words, to know true beauty, I must identify with Christ. Webster's dictionary defines identity as the "sameness of essential or generic character in different instances."[2] My identity is the core of who I am—the "sameness of essential . . . character"—a constant by which I am defined, regardless of circumstances. Identity in Christ, though, is not a passive understanding of our individual characteristics. Identity in Christ is a powerful, living force. My identity defines and shapes my life: "I have been crucified with Christ; it is no longer I who live, but Christ lives in me; and the life which I now live in the flesh I live by faith in the Son of God, who loved me and gave Himself for me" (Galatians 2:20). My understanding of physical beauty, along with the desires of my flesh, has been crucified with Christ. Thus the beauty that now resides in me is that of the Spirit, not of the flesh.

Furthermore, my body, along with my beauty, is now a symbol of my relationship with Jesus Christ. Paul set forth this idea when he wrote,

> For the love of Christ compels us, because we judge thus: that if One died for all, then all died; and He died for all, *that those who live should live no longer for themselves, but for Him who died for them and rose again*. (2 Corinthians 5:14–15, italics added)

My life is no longer about me. My beauty is no longer about me. Trying to create my own beauty in the world's image is to separate my beauty from my identity in Christ. Holding to the world's image of beauty is refusing to crucify my desires and living willfully in the flesh.

Two questions then arise: how do I live out my identity

in Christ, and how do I change my perspective from worldly beauty to spiritual beauty? After all, I am both flesh and spirit. I cannot simply say that how I look doesn't matter.

With one simple statement, Jesus summed up how we are to find our identity and our beauty in Him. When asked which commandment was the greatest, Jesus responded, "'You shall love the LORD your God with all your heart, with all your soul, and with all your mind.' This is the first and great commandment" (Matthew 22:37–38). When I pursue God with all I am, what I want will change. Worldly desire will die, and my new desire will be to live in Him and for Him. Finding my identity in Christ, I allow all that I am—spirit, mind, and body—to be defined by God.

God has given us the Holy Spirit to help us understand our new identity.

> For as many as are led by the Spirit of God, these are sons of God. For you did not receive the spirit of bondage again to fear, but you received the Spirit of adoption by whom we cry out, "Abba, Father." The Spirit Himself bears witness with our spirit that we are children of God. (Romans 8:14–16)

When we allow the Holy Spirit to direct us, we avoid becoming enslaved to the world's standard of beauty, and instead are set free to find our true beauty in Christ. When the Holy Spirit "bears witness . . . that we are children of God," we begin to see ourselves and our beauty as God sees us.

My understanding of beauty will then have proper

perspective because I will see myself not as the world sees me but as God sees me—in Christ.

Presenting our bodies as a sacrifice to God is but one element of what God desires to accomplish in us. The apostle Paul urged us to present our bodies a "living sacrifice, holy, acceptable to God, which is [our] reasonable service" (Romans 12:1). According to The New Bible Commentary, "This living sacrifice also includes the mind which, however, must first be renewed before it can be offered. This is a miracle of transformation, a readjustment to both temporal and eternal realities."[3]

Paul continued with these words:

> And do not be conformed to this world, but be transformed by the renewing of your mind, that you may prove what is that good and acceptable and perfect will of God. (Romans 12:2)

In other words, the key to finding my beauty is not in the transformation of my body, but in the transformation of my mind.

Thankfully, this mental transformation does not rely on my power. Again, God's Holy Spirit is available to give direction and wisdom.

> *"If you love Me, keep My commandments*. And I will pray the Father, and He will give you another Helper, that He may abide with you forever—*the Spirit of truth, whom the world cannot receive, because it neither sees Him nor knows Him;* but you know Him,

for He dwells with you and will be in you." (John
14:15–17, italics added)

To understand the role of the Holy Spirit in transforming
our thinking about beauty, we must realize that the Holy
Spirit is the Spirit of truth who will give us the discernment
to know the truth of God's beauty. What we hear will reveal
the heart of God and thus be in accord with the Word of
God. However, the Holy Spirit cannot be heard if we are
unwilling to listen to and live by God's commandments.
Nor can the Spirit reveal the truth of God's beauty if we
insist on viewing ourselves from a worldly perspective. The
Holy Spirit fulfills His role as our Counselor as we seek to
see ourselves and others from a godly perspective of beauty.

This transformation is a process not an event. It requires
daily renewal. To believers in the first-century church of
Ephesus, Paul wrote, "be renewed in the spirit of your mind,
and . . . put on the new man which was created according to
God, in true righteousness and holiness" (Ephesians
4:23–24). Being renewed in our minds requires action—we
are to "put on the new man." In another letter, this one to
believers in Corinth, Paul described the process as "bringing
every thought into captivity to the obedience of Christ"
(2 Corinthians 10:5).

In other words, I must *choose* to see myself as God sees
me. I must *choose* to consider all things in my life in light of
their spiritual importance. I must *choose* to set aside the
world's definition of beauty. Rather than evaluating
everything I eat in terms of what will make me fat or thin,
and instead of choosing to exercise to reach a certain

clothing size, I work to make choices for my body in terms
of what will bring strength and health to my temple that I
might accomplish the tasks God has for me to do. Rather
than making sure that my hair is in the right place, I ensure
that my heart is in the right place. Rather than worrying
that my jewelry doesn't match my outfit, I contemplate
whether my attitude matches what I profess to believe.
Rather than wondering if others see me as physically
beautiful, I focus on whether others see Christ's spiritual
beauty in me. But the process is not without struggle.

The greatest battle I face in allowing God to transform
my mind occurs when I see myself in pictures. Perhaps you
recognize the routine. You smile at seeing friends and loved
ones but find it difficult to smile at seeing yourself. Assess,
critique, reject. Without meaning to, you compare yourself
to others in the picture, perhaps wishing that you weren't
even in the photo. But when you wish away your presence,
you wish away the memory.

God continually reminds me that more important than
what I think of the way I look in a picture is the memory
the picture creates. Do you avoid cameras because your hair
doesn't look right, your clothes are too messy, or you feel
too fat? Don't cheat yourselves and others out of the legacy
of a memory because you're seeing yourself from the wrong
perspective.

Imagine a woman who goes to a store and buys a
beautiful pearl necklace. The jeweler places the necklace in a
small, plain cardboard box. Upon arriving home, the woman
proudly shows off her purchase. Without bothering to look
inside, her friends ooh and aah over the box and then spend

hours discussing how to decorate it with various ribbons and bows. Having seen the importance that her friends place on the box, the woman spends hours each day looking at it and wondering if it's as beautiful as another's. Eventually, she begins to wonder why the jeweler didn't give her a better box. Day after day, she complains about the inadequacy of her box and wishes that it were more valuable. But she never opens the box. The real beauty remains hidden, unappreciated, and unshared.

How ridiculous, we say. Yet God has placed a priceless treasure within us, and day after day we complain that the box it's in isn't made to our satisfaction. The real beauty remains hidden, unappreciated, and unshared.

My hair, face, and body tell others very little about my passions, dreams, and gifts. However, if my identity is in Christ, who I am on the inside will be visible in my actions. A life lived in the Spirit is marked by certain behaviors—the fruit of my life—not by my appearance: "But the fruit of the Spirit is love, joy, peace, longsuffering, kindness, goodness, faithfulness, gentleness, self-control. Against such there is no law" (Galatians 5:22–23).

Growing spiritual fruit requires a transformation of the mind because what I think and believe determine how I act:

> Anyone who listens to the word but does not do what it says is like a man who looks at his face in a mirror and, after looking at himself, goes away and immediately forgets what he looks like. But the man who looks intently into the perfect law that gives freedom, and continues to do this, not

> forgetting what he has heard, but doing it—he will
> be blessed in what he does. (James 1:23–25 NIV)

Accordingly, the more I study the Word *and put it into action*, the more I am transformed into the image of Christ. The more I pursue Christ, the more I see life in proper perspective.

A paradox of Scripture is that the more we bind ourselves to Christ, the more freedom we enjoy. Believing this paradox requires a shift in perspective. Enacting this paradox requires a shift in priorities. Cultivating the fruit of the Spirit requires work. Often we convince ourselves that changing physically is easier than developing spiritually. After all, a new hairstyle doesn't require that I find the weak areas of my character and allow God to push me to change. But a new hairstyle doesn't free me from the unrealistic expectations of worldly beauty. Neither does losing ten or fifteen pounds.

In contrast, a new perspective and new priorities make me free indeed. After listing the spiritual fruit that I am to cultivate, Paul added, "Against such there is no law." Tending to the growth of spiritual fruit takes me from slavery to freedom.

To find this freedom I must shift my perspective from the mirror of the world to the mirror of the Word. Trying to find beauty in the mirror of this world will leave me broken and lost. But losing myself in the mirror of the Word will reveal the greatest beauty ever known. After all, the Word is a mirror that reflects the very Truth that sets us free.

Allowing God to teach me how to love myself will

change not only my life but the lives of others as well. Jesus knew that loving God with all of our being would create a natural outpouring of love. After reaffirming the greatest commandment, He added, "And the second is like it: 'You shall love your neighbor as yourself'" (Matthew 22:39). Those of us who struggle to love ourselves are uncertain how to apply what we know about loving ourselves to the practice of loving others. Often our love for others is based on the need for affirmation and value. As such, our love for others is selfish. We intend to love others selflessly, but our own insecurities cause us to use people as a measure of our own significance. Since we eventually will find our identity in whatever gives us significance, we inappropriately remove our identity from Christ and find it in others. However, when I find my worth and identity in Christ, I am able to love others unselfishly because I am not concerned about what value they bring me or what worth they affirm in me. I love them for the value God has instilled in them.

Having worked in youth ministry for almost ten years, I have noticed several things about the female temperament. Girls are territorial. A young girl will gather her friends around her and silently dare anyone to disturb her social defense. While young men possess a relatively easygoing attitude toward friendships, girls build alliances and isolate enemies. To girls, friendships are a means of protection against the forces of insecurity.

Women are not much different. While our battles are quieter and usually more sophisticated, our walls of defense are thicker. Feeling the intensity of our own insecurities, we resist new friendships and feel threatened when our confidants open their lives to someone other than us. We may even abandon a friendship because we fear a shifting of allegiance. Emily Dickinson's poem "A Soul Selects Her Own Society" reveals her own exclusivity in relationships:

> I've known her—from an ample nation—
> Choose One—
> Then—close the Valves of her attention—
> Like Stone—[4]

While we can understand Dickinson's fear of rejection and betrayal, we also understand that such fear can render us powerless to love. Wittingly or unwittingly, we often choose friends based on the level of security they offer. Sometimes we even allow our insecurities to determine how we view other women.

However, when the Holy Spirit transforms our perspective regarding our beauty, our relationships with others change:

> And those who are Christ's have crucified the flesh with its passions and desires. If we live in the Spirit, let us also walk in the Spirit. Let us not become conceited, provoking one another, envying one another. (Galatians 5:24–26)

Rather than comparing ourselves to other women and becoming jealous, we see them through God's eyes and become grateful for their unique gifts and talents. Likewise, rather than being territorial about our friendships, we welcome new relationships as an opportunity to minister Christ's love more effectively.

When I see myself and others through God's eyes, my life, including my body, becomes an instrument of ministry that fulfills the purpose for which it was created—to bring glory and honor to an awesome God.

I must stay focused on things that are eternal even though I am living in a temporal world. What will matter more to my children: my wearing a size six or my exhibiting patience and gentleness with them? What will my husband value more in our marriage: my having firm breasts and toned buttocks or my exhibiting faithfulness and love for him? What has the power for greater ministry: my having flawless makeup and perfectly coordinated outfits or my cultivating kindness and self-control? Allowing the Holy Spirit to transform my mind enables God to use all of my life for His glory.

Seeing beauty requires a godly perspective. If I rely on my own understanding, I will never have the proper perspective. But when I trust the One on whom the whole earth rests, "the veil is taken away. Now the Lord is the Spirit; and where the Spirit of the Lord is, there is liberty. But we all, with unveiled face, beholding as in a mirror the glory of the Lord, are being transformed into the same image from glory to glory, just as by the Spirit of the Lord" (2 Corinthians 3:16b–18). The closer I move toward Him, the more accurate my perspective becomes.

LOOKING IN THE MIRROR
Personal Reflection

Identify one area of your understanding of beauty for which you need to hear the wisdom of the Holy Spirit.

How should the knowledge that your identity comes from Christ impact your perspective of your own beauty?

Being led by the Spirit is a daily discipline. In what ways should you daily "put on the new man who is renewed in knowledge according to the image of Him who created him" (Colossians 3:10)?

Think about your thoughts and actions as you go through your day. How do they relate to God's view of beauty?

Write down any thoughts or actions that need to change for your life to line up with a proper spiritual perspective of beauty.

Write down any thoughts or actions that reveal how the Holy Spirit is helping you to change your perspective.

Are there any relationships in your life that have been affected by your preoccupation and pursuit of the world's standard of beauty? Have any of your friendships with other women been shaped by your insecurities? Identify at least two of these relationships and explain how they've been affected by your own incorrect perceptions about beauty.

Read Philemon 6. Apply this Scripture to the relationships you identified in the question above. As you answer the question, remember that the real treasure resides in the box. Thus the real treasure of your life is not your physical appearance or your abilities but Christ in you.

Read Galatians 5:22–23. The level to which you heed the Holy Spirit will determine the harvest of the fruits of the Spirit in your life. In your time of prayer, ask the Lord to show you two fruits of the Spirit that He desires to produce in your life. While you must rely upon the wisdom of the Holy Spirit to direct the development of these fruits, you must play an active role as well. List specific actions you can take to cultivate the fruit that the Lord desires to produce in you.

$\mathscr{B}$ODY BY CHARIS

FITNESS experts who promise to recreate bodies with endless programs and products are a dime a dozen. But no workout program or wonder drug can reshape a woman's body more quickly and drastically than pregnancy. With little effort, and nine short (or long—depending on perspective) months, a woman's body undergoes more changes than she could ever imagine.

When I became pregnant with my first child, my initial thoughts were how cute and maternal I would look as my body grew rounder. I was thrilled when I could no longer button my pants. I wasn't bothered that my regular clothes began feeling snug when I was only in my eighth week. I was eager to begin wearing new maternity clothes, so I didn't fret about the thirty-two weeks still to come. Why worry about a few extra pounds? I would lose them in no time after the baby came.

At the end of my second trimester—now excessively bored with maternity clothes—I began to grapple with the evidence that my rear was expanding at an alarming rate, that my thighs were looking more like cottage cheese than cottage cheese, and that my breasts were drooping out of control. I may have looked cute with those maternity clothes on, but my naked self was another sight altogether. I began to wonder how my husband could possibly find me attractive—cute, maybe, with the clothes on—but attractive, much less sexy? No way, and especially not without the clothes!

When my husband told me I looked beautiful, I figured the idea of a baby's coming had warped his brain . . . and his vision. Even though I reveled in his compliments and gazes, I couldn't quite shake the fear that he was delusional. As the remaining weeks passed, and my body continued to grow, the upcoming arrival and my euphoric visions of motherhood kept me distracted. Besides, I had other tasks to attend to—trying to shave my legs when I couldn't quite see them, navigating my way through tight spaces, and desperately seeking (but never quite finding) a comfortable sleeping position. When those tiny little voices reminded me of my enlarged body (as if I needed reminding), I consoled myself with the knowledge that I was pregnant—and that I would lose those baby pounds as soon as the baby came.

The day finally arrived when we welcomed our daughter into the world. Never does a woman feel quite so thin as when she drops eight to ten pounds of baby and amniotic fluid. Even seeing my body in a full-length mirror didn't diminish the lightness I felt. The rolls and sags were still there (along with some new ones), and my rear end—well, it was definitely still there. But I felt like a new woman. I could bend over, I could shave my legs, and I could breathe. I felt svelte.

But feelings come and go like hormones rise and fall. In the early stages of nursing, I wondered how something so natural could be so difficult. But my daughter and I pressed onward. I told myself that she and I would both benefit from the struggle. She would receive the best nourishment possible, and I would return to my pre-pregnancy weight. Basking in the glow of motherhood, which brought a fleeting burst of energy, I began exercising again.

Three weeks into my new life, reality settled in to stay. Exercising fell by the wayside as I realized the demands of keeping up with a newborn. Nursing became much easier but failed to provide the weight-loss promised by so many baby books and magazines.

My life had changed; my body had changed.

Amid the seemingly millions of diapers and the exhausting late-night feedings, the time soon came to set aside the maternity clothes. However, I had a slight dilemma (if a woman's dilemma with her wardrobe could ever be termed "slight"). I was ready to pack away the maternity clothes, but I had lost only ten of the thirty-five pounds I had gained, and going naked was out of the question. I had to choose between holding on to the fantasy of losing those baby pounds soon or facing the reality that, while the new life within me had separated from my body, much of the pregnancy weight remained.

The challenge was not simply to find clothes that fit my

reshaped body but also to find an identity that fit the new, maternal me. Who was I and how did I view the new me? My concept of love had expanded the moment I embraced the new little one who won my heart immediately. I loved all of her without reserve. But the struggle to love all of me was the same—a struggle. How could I look at myself and feel both overwhelming joy at who I was becoming as a mom and overwhelming dissatisfaction with what had happened to my body?

Realizing that the clothes fairy would not appear any time soon, and that my discontent was compounded by my clothing dilemma, I enlisted the moral support of a friend, and we went shopping for some new, larger clothes. Armed with a little extra money and the willpower of a woman with nothing to wear, I prepared myself for the challenge that lay ahead.

We ate lunch at a quiet restaurant before beginning to shop. Tucked away in the safety of the booth, away from dressing room mirrors and size tags, I shared with my friend the work God had begun in my life regarding my self-image. On and on I prated about my desire to be free from the world's definition of beauty and about my new determination to find my beauty in the woman God had created me to be.

But what I didn't share with her was the duality within me. I believed God had begun a good work in me by showing me how vastly different His definition of beauty is from the world's. The feelings of inadequacy and self-hatred that had bound me for so long were beginning to dissolve in the presence of God's love and grace. But the idols remained in the standards I still held. The struggle to see my beauty continued. I was still banking on one day losing those pregnancy pounds, and more. Then, I believed, I could feel completely confident being the person God created me to be.

Talking about accepting myself was easy to do as I munched on French bread and seafood quiche. But embracing my body and accepting myself were brutally difficult when I saw my reflection in the dressing room mirrors and storefront windows. At some point, however, for truth to be established, ideology and reality must kiss.

Beginning my shopping endeavors, I decided against trying on any pants since finding some casual dresses for work was more important. However, the urge soon overcame me. I decided to try on a pair of jeans just to see what size I wore. Passing by my ordinary size twelve relaxed fit, I also passed by the fourteens and the sixteens, coming to a meditative pause in front of size eighteen. Putting on my most optimistic look, I picked up a pair and headed for the dressing room, baby in tow. I had tried to prepare myself for the view, but I was not prepared for what I saw: each stretch mark and each extra inch from every angle imaginable. But with hope still in my heart, I forged on, hoping against hope that my body would undergo a miraculous transformation the moment the jeans hit my ankles.

As I gently, then vigorously, tugged the jeans up my legs, I was disheartened by the view in the mirror. I still looked like a postpartum mom, only now I had jeans painted to my legs. Slowly I peeled off the jeans, feeling my pride being stripped away at the same time. I sighed as I stepped back into my maternity stretch pants.

As I placed the pair of jeans back on the shelf, the saleswoman asked me if I had found what I was looking for.

Not unless the jeans come with a new body, I thought. Instead I said, "No thanks. I'm going to wait a little longer before buying jeans."

She understood immediately. "I owned at least twenty pairs of jeans before my son came," she said encouragingly. "After he was born I didn't fit into any of them. Everyone kept telling me the weight would come off quickly if I nursed. It didn't. But then when he hit five months, the weight all came off, and I could fit into all of my jeans."

Two thoughts crossed my mind: *You don't look like you've had a fat day in your life* and *There's still hope for me*.

I clung to the latter. I still had three months before Charis would be five months old. Maybe I was rushing things. So my friend and I headed off to find some casual dresses.

Finding two surprisingly stylish jumpers that would hide all stretch marks and breast-milk leaks, I considered our shopping foray a relative success. After all, eventually the weight would come off, and I would be able to wear my good old comfortable size twelve jeans.

However, several months after Charis was born, I was no closer to a size twelve than I had been twenty minutes after giving birth. Feeling my old foe creeping up behind me, I asked God to continue the good work He had begun. I continued to struggle, but therein lay my hope. I struggled, I wrestled, I would not give in.

Prior to giving birth to my daughter, I thought my struggle with self-esteem was mostly in the past. But in the added, unexpected time of wrestling, I learned that learning to love my body is a journey. Understanding God's beauty is a process. Watching my body change through the gift of childbirth was simply one leg of the journey. My life had changed; my body had changed; but God had not. Pregnancy changed my body; motherhood would transform my mind.

I had given birth—brought forth life from my body—and I wanted to see myself as my daughter saw me. I knew I needed to let motherhood change my definition of beauty. If I failed to allow it to do so, I would rob myself of the joys of motherhood.

More important, God had brought forth life from my body, and I needed to see myself as God saw me.

During this time, I discovered two key concepts regarding my beauty. First, my body had performed an amazing feat in bringing forth life. Christian women know that children are a gift from the Lord, but rarely do we connect this truth with our own bodies. As Israel's king David said, "Behold, children are a heritage from the LORD, the fruit of the womb is a reward" (Psalm 127:3). However, after giving birth we quickly disconnect the wonder of childbirth from the stretch marks that mar our once smooth skin.

Unlike modern women, the ancient psalmist David recognized and revered the creation process:

> For You formed my inward parts;
> You covered me in my mother's womb.

I will praise You, for I am fearfully and wonderfully
made;
Marvelous are Your works,
And that my soul knows very well.
My frame was not hidden from You,
When I was made in secret,
And skillfully wrought in the lowest parts of the
earth.
Your eyes saw my substance, being yet unformed.
 And in Your book they all were written,
The days fashioned for me,
When as yet there were none of them.
(Psalm 139:13–16)

In his commentary on Psalms, Charles Spurgeon
discussed the intricate link we have with God in the
moment of our creation:

There I lay hidden—covered by Thee. Before I could
know Thee, or aught else, Thou hadst a care for me,
and didst hide me away as a treasure . . . Thus the
Psalmist describes the intimacy which God had
with him . . . [Y]et unborn, he was under the
control and guardianship of God.[1]

The moment we were created we became God's most
precious and coveted work of art—chosen, guarded, and
loved. As a woman of God, I must recognize that I am
"fearfully and wonderfully" made because I am a product of
the creative hand of the Most High God. I am "fearfully and

wonderfully" made because I have access to one of the greatest intimacies humans can know—a personal relationship with God.

The word *fearful* often makes us think of someone who is anxious and afraid. But placed in the context of God's abilities, the word takes on new meaning. When we are fearful of the work of God, we gaze with absolute attention and awe at the possibilities that exist in the very palm of His hand. Thus, I become totally fixed on God and His purpose for my life instead of being distracted and weighed down by the culture of our world.

Being fearful of the work of God means realizing that the possibilities for my life extend far beyond what I am able to bring about on my own. They exist in the abilities of an infinite God. And if the possibilities for my life exist in the abilities of an infinite God, I must define who I was at the moment of creation, who I am today, and who I will be tomorrow as God defines me, that is "fearfully and wonderfully made." I must declare as the psalmist did, "Marvelous are Your works, and that my soul knows very well." Deep within me are these words, which long to be heard over the din of this world. I was created by a perfect and flawless Creator, He intimately and deeply loves me, and I can rest with contentment in who I am in Christ Jesus.

So what does this discussion have to do with stretch marks and excess cellulite?

When I understand the mighty work of God's creative nature in giving me life, I can begin to understand the formidable and awe-inspiring task my body has completed in bringing forth a life that God has both ordained and created. When a woman carries a child, God doesn't see her rolling figure and say, "Oh my goodness, look at the size of her." Instead, He sees to the depths of her womb, hears the heartbeat of her child, and ponders this child's destiny. Why then do we look upon the body that has provided nourishment, warmth, and protection for such a life and reject the physical reminders of this experience?

While pregnant I had a discussion with a coworker expressing my confidence that my body would return to its pre-pregnancy state. "No, it won't," she stated unequivocally. "Your body will never return to what it was before this baby. But it won't make any difference to your husband. He'll still see your body as beautiful. Maybe even as more beautiful because your body is the one that gave him this child."

I understand her wisdom far better now than I did then. She was right about my figure. She was right about my husband. Motherhood changes everything. Even your concept of beauty. Even your husband's concept of beauty.

Second, I discovered, strangely enough, that my husband finds me more beautiful now than when I was forty pounds lighter. I find this difficult to believe. Because I am skeptical, I have difficulty letting my husband live this truth. Over the past few years, though, I've learned that when I place my husband in the box labeled "society's view of males," I underestimate who he really is and who he has the capacity to be in Christ.

In her article "Body Blues," writer Holly Robinson addressed a woman's incredulity at believing herself beautiful despite the extra weight:

Baby weight—those extra pounds that stick around
long after pregnancy—is a source of great
frustration for many new moms. And it's not just
the thought of squeezing into a swimsuit that
disturbs us. More unsettling are the deep-seated
fears that a post baby body will make us
unappealing sexually. After all, we wonder, is there
anything attractive about stretch marks, a flabby
stomach, and drooping breasts? . . . But the fact is
that most men really don't care if a woman's butt is
bigger or her belly is rounder. . . . One new dad,
whose wife has lost only 16 of the 60 pounds she
gained during pregnancy, agrees: "How my wife
looks hasn't affected my desire for her at all. I love
her even more because she's such a good mother."
Frequently, women find sentiments like this hard to
believe—and no wonder. We are surrounded by
media images that equate sexuality with young,
trim, toned bodies, and a maternal figure is often
presented as decidedly unsexy.[2]

Christian women know that sexuality extends far deeper
than the physical. Or, at least, we should know. Author
Cathy Winks says that a woman's sexuality "is less about
slinky dresses and more about having a powerful body that
can do wonderful things."[3] After all, "stretch marks, flabby
stomach, and drooping breasts" are reminders not only of
the creative act of God within my body, but also of the deep
intimacy that exists between me and my husband.

Often, though, our own insecurities hinder our

relationships with our husbands. We see thin, young models in magazines and know without a doubt that our excess cellulite, tired eyes, and spit-up-scented hair can't compete. We convince ourselves that our husbands, while making love to us, imagine being with younger, thinner, better-smelling versions of ourselves. While we treasure these moments of intimacy, they are tinged with sad imaginings of what we aren't. Meanwhile, our husbands are simply enjoying us—just as we are, not as we want ourselves to be.

A woman who understands her beauty in Christ will allow her husband not only to see her changing body as beautiful but also give him the freedom to tell her that he sees her body as beautiful. She will not reject his advances on the basis of her own misconceptions of what she thinks he wants. In her article "Will I Ever Have Sex Again?" Robinson wrote,

> The sad truth is that women are more likely than men to buy into the idea that skinny and young is the only way to be sexy. . . . As new dad Bob Snyder says, "I didn't realize how having a baby would dramatically change the way my wife felt about herself sexually. And what she didn't realize was that to me, she was as beautiful on the day we got home from the hospital as she's ever been, because she is my beauty, my bride, and my love."[4]

As a woman of God, I must trust the heart of my husband and believe him when he tells me that he desires me. I am the woman he chose, forsaking all others. I must let him continue to choose me—just as I am—for he is my beloved and I am his.

Look into the eyes of the child who bears the image of you and your beloved, and rejoice in the mighty work of God. Compared to the great destiny of motherhood, your changed body is of little consequence. Do not spend your days wishing you were someone else while your child sits nearby, looking into your face and desiring no mother but you.

LOOKING IN THE MIRROR
Personal Reflection

Do you believe that you are "fearfully and wonderfully" made? Why or why not?

Read Romans 9:20. Paraphrase this Scripture in relation to how you view your body.

How do your struggles with self-image affect your relationship with your husband physically and emotionally?

Do you believe your husband when he tells you that you are beautiful? Why or why not?

Do you assess your husband according to the world's standard for men, either by expecting him to look like the world's image of manhood or by expecting him to think and act as the world does? If your answer is yes, how have these assessments affected your relationship with your husband?

In what ways do your feelings toward yourself about your body affect your relationships with your children?

What do you long for your children to understand about beauty?

How do you want your understanding of God's perspective of beauty to affect your relationship with your husband?

As you ask the Lord to accomplish these things in your life, remember the words of God spoken through the prophet Jeremiah: "Behold I am the LORD, the God of all flesh. Is there anything too hard for Me?" (32:27).

··· EIGHT ···

$\mathcal{T}$HE MODEL FIGURE

LIKE it or not, you're being watched. Mother or not, you're being watched. If you could pass on any inheritance to the next generation of women what would it be?

The effect of media on women is undeniable, but I question whether we really understand the extent to which we've been seduced by the world's message. We look at a teenager with baggy pants or multiple piercings and tattoos and say that her appearance reflects worldly values. But what about the Christian woman who colors and styles her hair like a popular actress and who longs to look like a *Vogue* model? The principle is the same.

We do ourselves and our young women a great disservice when we ignore not only the mirror of youth culture but also the mirror of our own. As a youth pastor's wife, I have become more and more disheartened with the challenges I face with teenage girls in regard to modesty. Yet I understand that they, like me, are influenced by their own culture and by their need to feel personal worth—even if it means being reduced to an object.

When I see teenage girls equating beauty with society's standards, I begin to look at what the women in the church offer as an alternative. Unfortunately, I see mothers who willingly purchase immodest clothing so that their daughters can fit in, women who push the standards of modesty themselves, and women who may not dress immodestly but who have no sense of what beauty should mean to the Christian woman.

We know from modern psychology that insecurity about body image is one of the markers of the onset of adolescence. Sadly, concerns about physical appearance seem to be interrupting childhood innocence earlier and earlier. Concerns once associated with young women in high school now invade the thoughts of girls as young as seven and eight who obsess over their weight and appearance.

In *Reviving Ophelia: Saving the Selves of Adolescent Girls*, Mary Pipher examined the impact of culture upon the emotional and mental development of young girls. She has sounded a much-needed alarm about the destructive forces of culture on adolescent girls. Discussing the overwhelming dissatisfaction girls feel toward their bodies, she wrote,

> Just at the point that their bodies are becoming rounder, girls are told that thin is beautiful, even imperative. Girls hate the required gym classes in

which other girls talk about their fat thighs and stomachs. One girl told me of showering next to an eighty-five-pound dancer who was on a radical diet. For the first time in her life she looked at her body and was displeased.[1]

Pipher's research struck a personal note when a mom at our church shared with me her daughter's frustration with the atmosphere in the girls' locker room at her high school. After gym class, girls would often pick up one another's clothing to see what size their peers wore. While this mother monitored the media her daughter consumed, she was unable to protect her from the impact of the world's expectations—even in the environment of a Christian school.

Although their research was conducted at least ten years apart and in different professional capacities, clinical psychologist Mary Pipher and youth culture expert Paul Robertson come to the same conclusion regarding the influence of media on young teenage girls. Pipher spoke not only from her professional experience with adolescent girls, but also from personal experience as a mother:

Teen magazines are a good example of the training in "lookism" that girls receive. While waiting at a drugstore to pick up a prescription, I leafed through some magazines. The models all looked six feet tall and anorexic. The emphasis was on makeup, fashion, and weight. Girls were encouraged to spend money and to diet and work out in order to develop the looks that would attract boys. Apparently attracting boys was the sole purpose of life, because the magazines had no articles on careers, hobbies, politics or academic pursuits. I couldn't find one that wasn't preaching the message, "Don't worry about feeling good or being good, worry about looking good."[2]

Not much has changed since 1994. While society may be more aware of the prevalence and dangers of eating disorders, we continue to bow down to the idol of being thin.

Robertson spent "numerous hours sifting through [an] issue of *Seventeen*, leaving no ad or article unexamined." He asserted that

[t]he power media has to dictate values and standards continues to grow. Our kids spend hundreds of hours every year with their media heroes and spend billions trying to look like them. Young girls are influenced by unattainable, airbrushed standards of beauty that even the cover girls themselves never achieve.[3]

At one of the most impressionable times in life, young girls are being lured by an elusive and empty ideal and told to use it as a model for their bodies and their lives.

Pipher's and Robertson's research confirmed what I had experienced as a youth pastor's wife and high school educator, but I wanted to look further to see if it reflected the experiences of students in our youth ministry. My casual and unscientific research supported the concern that our teenagers are picking up troubling messages. When asked what messages the media send regarding a woman's value and beauty, they responded:.

"You have to be beautiful to be anything." (female)

"That she cares more about acceptance of others than acceptance of [herself]." (male)

"Magazines and T.V. believe a woman who shows skin is sexy and beautiful." (female)

"Body only." (male)

"A woman has to have certain size breasts . . . A woman cannot be overweight, or too skinny, but just 'perfect.' A woman must wear makeup and wear revealing clothing to be 'beautiful.'" (female)

"[I]t totally has to do with how sexy you are." (female)

A prime concern of teenage girls is their relationships with the opposite sex. Well aware of this concern, editors of teen magazines attract readers with articles offering sure-fire advice for any young woman hoping to catch the boy of her dreams. Exploiting this same idea, although at times more subtle in their approach, advertisers use pictures to create the idea that products guarantee popularity as well as happiness. Many ads selling products for women picture men. Sometimes they are only in the background; other times they are featured in very physical, often sexual poses. More often than not, the men are bare-chested, and they are always models of cultural perfection. These advertisers perpetuate not only the ideal that young females are expected to be physically perfect but that they are to desire physically perfect males as well.

Anyone looking at teen magazines will find the same messages that Pipher and Robertson reported. *Cosmogirl!* features headlines and sub-headlines such as "Find Your Perfect Look" and "Hollywood's Hottest Hairstyles."[4] Even *Girls Life Magazine*, which is geared toward preteens, offers articles such as "You! Only Better . . . The New Look You Have to Try" and advertisements for products "that will brighten your life, make you happy, and help you have fun and look great."[5] From beginning to end, readers face a barrage of products promising to make young girls more beautiful, more popular, and thus happier. Overwhelmingly absent from these magazines was the discussion of character development.

Disheartened by the emphasis on external beauty in teen magazines, I had a glimmer of hope when I read the headline: "Soul Search: How to Be Pretty on the Inside"[6] in *Seventeen* magazine. Flipping to the article, however, I was disappointed to find a list of steps for yoga, three quotes from readers regarding prayer, and instructions on following a "walking exercise . . . [to be] taken at sunset, meant to connect [the reader] to the power of the earth." This article not only left inner beauty undefined, but also ignored the inherent longing of every woman, young and old, to know and to achieve true beauty.

When I was a teenager, the cultural ideal for young women was to be thin, have beautiful hair and makeup, and wear fashionable clothing. Today's cultural mores are similar, but the stakes are much higher. If we are to believe what we read, a young girl's sexual appeal is the measure of her beauty. Either we've forgotten the true meaning of the word *sexy* or society intends for young girls to be judged according to their ability to be sexual. The casual use of this word, and the subtle and not-so-subtle references to the act it refers to, astounded me. Young girls can open the pages of *Cosmogirl!* to find out how to "Get Sexy Hair Now!"[7] Or they can look in *TeenVogue* to find makeup tips in an article titled "Peep Show: Spring's Bold Eye Makeup Is Sure to Get You Noticed."[8] To find garments that repel rain but not guys, she could read *Seventeen* magazine's feature on "The Perfect Storm: Slick and Sexy Rainy-day Clothes." Turning back several pages, she could discover "3 Steps to Sexy Hair."[9] To say that a person looks sexy is to say that she is desirable for sex. Moreover, it is to suggest that she is available for sex. Is this the message we want young girls to hear?

Not only are girls expected to recognize and use their sexuality to achieve acceptance, they are also to recognize and affirm the sexuality of their male counterparts. In the same issue of *Cosmogirl!*, readers were to vote as to the male who would "be on the cover of [their] 'Sexiest Guys in the World' issue."[10] This same magazine includes a male pin-up each month as well as a feature where girls can rate a male based on his physical appearance. According to this perspective, males and females are valuable if they evoke a sexual response.

Advertisers follow suit with their references to sex to sell products. A popular teen store in our mall had a storefront display that read, "Today's sexiest jeans are now next to nothing."[11] While the term "next to nothing" was an obvious reference to the price, the picture was a perverse play on words as a woman dressed only in jeans and an open denim jacket stood in the arms of a bare-chested man in jeans. The same store later featured a window display showing a female model with her shirt completely unbuttoned and the sides of her breasts showing. The caption read, "Pussycat by day, Man-eater by night."[12]

Jean companies are some of the worst offenders in using sex to sell their products. Ad after ad in teen magazines features women in overtly sexual clothing and poses. While today's hip-hugger jeans push the standards of modesty, one company goes even further to advertise "adjustable low rise jeans." The fifth step in adjusting the jeans reads, "Pull down to desired level or 'effect.'" The ad includes the warning: "Try this only at home. Do not attempt to lower too much. Doing so will result in nudity."[13] Sometimes, the very product itself is lost in the advertisement of sexuality.

Robertson voiced concern that "*Seventeen* and other similar magazines, [sic] reduce our girls to the sum total of what they wear, how they smell and what makeup they use."[14]

I would go a step further and say that today's magazines

and advertising campaigns "reduce our girls to the sum total" of their sexuality. Most frightening to me is the realization that while physical perfection remains an elusive ideal for young girls, sexual exhibitionism and promiscuity are not.

As if advertisements and magazine articles weren't enough to promulgate the idea that sexuality is beauty, many popular female artists and actresses—the very ones who serve as role models for young girls today—perpetuate the same idea.

An interview with music artist Christina Aguilera on ABC's *20/20* illustrated the way icons of culture are moving to a more sexually explicit definition of beauty. In her introduction to the interview, Barbara Walters identified Aguilera's "new act" as "dirty and beautiful." According to Walters, Aguilera was "shedding her old image and much of her clothes."[15]

Hating the "pop princess" label, Aguilera explained that she had deliberately made these changes because she needed to be true to herself. For Aguilera, being true to herself meant stripping away pretense and baring her soul by exposing her body. Ironically, her song "Beautiful" argues against the cultural perceptions that objectify women.

Having studied the impact of Aguilera's music on teens today, youth culture expert Walt Mueller wrote the following in reference to Aguilera's song "Beautiful":

> Released as a single and video, the slow and engaging ballad has been grasped by kids—female and male alike—who feel physically inadequate and

> struggling with issues of body image. The message . . .
> is simple and straightforward: you are a beautiful
> person no matter what anyone says.[16]

While we in the church often mouth the same sentiment, Aguilera puts a different spin on its meaning. The message of Aguilera's video and lifestyle is: a woman's beauty lies in her ability to be sexually provocative and to engage in sexual experimentation.

Interlaced with the provocative images of the new act, and Aguilera's bold assertions that she's happy with who she is, are references to the abuse she suffered from her father and his subsequent physical and emotional abandonment. I wonder if she sees any connection between her aggressive sexuality and her lack of relationship with her father. Aguilera said, "I never wanted to feel helpless to a man." The overt sexuality that she sees as "just me being me" seems to be an attempt to control men by exploiting her own body.

Responding to the criticism that her new perspective is inappropriate for someone who is a role model for young teenage girls, Aguilera said, "I think it scares people when a woman is comfortable with herself, her sexuality."

The audience she reaches, however, is not all women, and while she's "having fun and express[ing] herself" at age twenty-one, her fans include those who have yet to reach their preteen years.

At the end of the interview, the commentator asserted that Christina Aguilera has "perhaps redefined what it meant to be beautiful" and that Aguilera is "confident that no matter what people say, she knows what it means to be beautiful." Barbara Walters closed the segment by saying, in reference to Aguilera's success with her new song "Dirty," "The new image hasn't hurt Christina's career. Good for her."[17]

Good for her? Is this the best response that older women in society have to offer young girls today?

The world is all too ready to plant its philosophies regarding women and beauty in the hearts of young girls. The voices are many but the message is the same: a girl's sexuality is her beauty. However, it is a message of death. Satan desires to destroy the hearts of young girls through the destruction of their bodies.

Sadly, the Christian community's response has been woefully inadequate. As a youth pastor's wife, I have heard many women express their dismay, and others their outrage, at the lack of modesty in young women's clothing. While I wholeheartedly agree that we have a standard of modesty to uphold, we've lost our ability to communicate this message to young girls. Too many times, we say, "Don't dress that way," and expect our admonition to be enough. However, if we have no other standard of beauty to offer and no instruction by which they can learn their value in Christ, we cannot expect them to see the destructive force of the world's standards.

Perhaps we are unable to counter the world's assertions about beauty because we are too busy buying into the same messages. Although older women may not struggle with the issues of sexuality and immodesty that young girls face, we still strive to achieve the world's standard of beauty.

Whether or not we are prepared for it, we are models for the young women around us. If they see us desiring to look like the world, they will continue their pursuit of the world's acceptance and affirmation—sexuality and all.

My husband and I once had the opportunity to go out to dinner with a young, female Christian recording artist. After releasing two CDs, and touring nationally with other well-known artists, she came face to face with the idealistic view even Christians have about beauty. Walking into an airline terminal, she was greeted by the party assigned to pick her up. Upon seeing her, the person exclaimed how different she looked from her CD cover. In retrospect, she laughed at the disappointment, but she expressed disbelief that anyone would actually expect her to look like an airbrushed picture at all times. "They even airbrushed out part of my hips," she chuckled, referring to the production company.

I knew that touch-up work for CD cover photos was common, but I couldn't believe the extent of it—especially in a recording company featuring Christian artists. Why do Christians uphold the world's vision of beauty in the way we package and market CDs, books, magazines, and conferences meant to be used as tools of ministry? Why can't we allow women to be their natural, beautiful selves?

We do not teach teenage girls the truth of God's beauty by showing them how to apply makeup and coordinate outfits or by encouraging them to abstain from such things. Instead we must teach them that their beauty resides in their souls. We must teach them that their bodies are the temple of the living God, and that their true beauty can be marred and lost by what they do with their bodies.

Why aren't we angry at the destruction Satan wreaks in the lives of young women? When will we rise out of our own pit of insecurity, lay hold to the truth of God's beauty in our own lives, and passionately plant this message in the lives of young girls? Rather than striving to achieve a model figure, we need to be the model figure.

Those of us who are mothers must realize that our daughters, and our sons, are watching and listening. They see how we respond to our own beauty, and they will model what they see. If we understand our true source of beauty, we are in a position to help our daughters hear the message.

Media are not the only influence on our children, as Nicole Johnson has pointed out:

> When your twelve-year-old, ninety-pound daughter starts obsessing about her weight or wanting to go on a diet, something is wrong. It may not be completely the world's fault. Yes, they do go to school, and they are bombarded by the same media that we are, but do we model love and acceptance ourselves? If we reject ourselves or our beauty, we'd better get ready to see our daughters do the same.[18]

If we continually deride our own looks and abilities, how can our daughters believe us when we tell them they are beautiful and that God has a plan for their lives? Likewise, whatever messages about beauty that we live out in our homes, our sons will carry out with them. If we expect and try to achieve physical perfection, how can we teach our sons to value and love the soul of a woman more than her shell?

Every Christian woman is a role model to the young women around her. We cannot avoid our responsibility by saying that we are not gifted to work with children or teenagers. God provides the wisdom and ability to live out His message of beauty through the power of the Holy Spirit. Before ascending into heaven, Jesus reminded the disciples of that provision when He said, "But you shall receive power when the Holy Spirit has come upon you; and you shall be witnesses to Me in Jerusalem, and in all Judea and Samaria, and to the end of the earth" (Acts 1:8). The empowerment of the Holy Spirit is available not only to explain salvation to potential believers but also to proclaim the things God is doing in our daily lives. We don't have to wonder how we will speak the truth—the Holy Spirit will anoint us to express the good news of God's life-giving beauty.

We must, however, take the time to build relationships. It is easy to stand on the sidelines and criticize the choices of the generations that follow. When we respond to young women by loving them and by investing in their lives, they will respond to the words that we speak.

Consider the relationship between Elizabeth, the mother of John the Baptist, and Mary, the mother of Jesus. Mary was an adolescent girl at a critical juncture in life. After receiving the angel's message, she sought the companionship of an older, trusted relative. The bond between Elizabeth and Mary put Elizabeth in a position to be used by God in Mary's life. Scripture doesn't tell us that Elizabeth was trained in how to communicate with adolescents. She simply followed God and that was enough.

Elizabeth and her husband "were both righteous before

God, walking in all the commandments and ordinances of the Lord blameless" (Luke 1:6). When the opportunity came for Elizabeth to speak, the Holy Spirit prompted her in what to say:

> And it happened, when Elizabeth heard the greeting of Mary, that the babe leaped in her womb; and Elizabeth *was filled with the Holy Spirit*. Then she spoke out with a loud voice and said, "Blessed are you among women, and blessed is the fruit of your womb!" (Luke 1:41–42, italics added)

Elizabeth didn't argue with God by insisting that she had nothing in common with an adolescent girl. She simply spoke the words the Holy Spirit inspired.

Upon hearing Mary's greeting, the child Elizabeth carried leaped in her womb, and Elizabeth cried out, "Blessed are you among women, and blessed is the fruit of your womb!" Elizabeth later said, "Blessed is she who believed, for there will be a fulfillment of those things which were told her from the Lord" (Luke 1:45). Elizabeth recognized that the child Mary carried in her womb was the Savior of the world; she saw with spiritual eyes that Mary carried the imperishable Seed.

Women today do not literally carry the Christ child within us, but we do carry the imperishable seed of Christ. We have "been born again, not of corruptible seed but incorruptible, through the word of God which lives and abides forever" (1 Peter 1:23). When we become believers, God plants the imperishable Seed of the Word in us and births the ministry of Christ in our lives. The active power of the Holy Spirit in our lives should leap within us as we recognize the seed present in the lives of the young women who surround us.

Generations of young girls need the love and mentorship of women who passionately desire to know and live out God's beauty. We cannot completely protect our daughters from the influence of culture, but we can recognize and acknowledge their true beauty and ours. The message begins in our homes, our churches, and our communities. The message begins with us. If we do not take up the cause and lead young women to an intimate understanding of God's design for their lives, an all-too-ready culture will sweep them into chaos.

We are naïve to expect culture to heed our voices of dismay and change the message it sends. Our voices are but a whisper in the clamor of the world. But the odds against us don't change the mandate. Love the young women around you and speak truth into their lives. Do not be discouraged. We travel this road to true beauty together. And when life brings unexpected turns in our journey, do not fear, for within our whisper is a Whisper.

LOOKING IN THE MIRROR
Personal Reflection

What messages do you see popular media sending young women? Give specific examples.

What evidence do you see that the messages are getting through to the young women you interact with?

Why is the message that a woman's beauty comes from her sexuality dangerous for women, young and old alike, to believe?

How does the over-sexualization of women affect girls who have not yet reached adolescence?

What messages regarding beauty do well-known Christians convey to young women through words and actions?

Consider the story of Ruth, a young woman willing to leave behind all that was familiar to her, take up residence in a foreign land, and live among people with whom she had no prior relationship (other than her mother-in-law, Naomi). Ruth said to her mother-in-law,

> Entreat me not to leave you,
> Or to turn back from following after you;
> For wherever you go, I will go;
> And wherever you lodge, I will lodge;

> Your people shall be my people,
> And your God, my God.
> Where you die, I will die,
> And there will I be buried.
> The LORD do so to me, and more also,
> If anything but death parts you and me.
> (Ruth 1:16–17)

God was more important to Ruth than her own familiar culture because she believed that Naomi's God was the One true God, and she believed this because she saw the Spirit of the living God active in Naomi's life.

If we want young women to believe that God is more important than culture, what must they see in us?

How did Naomi's willingness to mentor Ruth affect redemptive history? (See Ruth 4:17 and Matthew 1:5–6, 16.)

When it comes to understanding God's definition of beauty can you say to the young women around you "Imitate me, just as I also imitate Christ" (1 Corinthians 11:1) and "Hold fast the pattern of sound words which you have heard from me, in faith and love which are in Christ Jesus" (2 Timothy 1:13)? What lessons regarding beauty are you teaching through your words and actions?

BOUT FACE

HER name is beauty. Making our rounds of pastoral
visits, my husband and I walk into her room on the sixth
floor of the local hospital. We've heard that she is in
considerable pain. As we step through the doorway, we
catch sight of her across the room. She has just settled into a
chair with the help of a nurse who leaves the room as we
enter. I have come prepared to encourage her and to pray
with her, but I am unprepared for what I see.

Her beauty amazes me.

Dressed in the "ever-stylish" hospital gown, she wears no
makeup and her hair is uncombed. Her nausea has just
begun to subside. The pain is still present. Yet the beauty
surrounding her leaves me with a lasting impression. I bend
down next to her chair. I look at her and say, "You look
beautiful. And I mean that."

She responds with a wry smile, as if to say, "Yeah, right."

Her disbelief in her own beauty goes much deeper than anxiety about her hospital gown and disheveled look. In order to defeat the cancer invading her body, she has just had both of her breasts removed. Wrestling with the question of how this change will affect her life, she feels anything but beautiful. In a society where breasts are considered a defining feature of female beauty, her self-image has been inexorably altered.

She has lost the place where her children nestled as babies. Is she still a woman? She has lost a part of her body that helped to define her sexuality. Is she still a woman? She has lost the sense of control over her own body as it wars within itself. Is she still a woman?

I have never looked at an individual recovering from surgery and sensed such a presence of beauty. Her beauty is not that of a well-coordinated outfit, stylish hairdo, or perfect makeup. And yet beauty is undeniably there. As I tell her she is beautiful, my husband says, "I was just thinking the same thing." Of course, she doesn't believe him either. She thinks we are just trying to make her feel better. But later that evening, as we discuss our visit, we both marvel at the beauty we saw in her.

In one of her moments of greatest weakness God chose to reveal Himself through her. The Holy Spirit whispered, "Speak what you see."

I see beauty.

She leans against her Savior, and she finds grace. Knowing that only God can sustain her, she stands in the face of fear and resolves not to give up. She recognizes that the things of God are the only things that matter. Seeking the things of Christ, she lives a life of integrity. She is a fighter, a survivor, a woman of strength.

She is beauty.

HER name is beauty. Housewife, mother of two, tall and slender. She doesn't seem to wrestle with her own sense of self worth. But she questions her beauty.

Twelve years of marriage. One day he decides to leave. Another woman. Broken promises, broken marriage, broken heart.

A few weeks after he leaves, she and I cross paths in a bookstore. "I feel like I've lived a lie," she says, tears gently rolling down her cheeks. "All these months, and I didn't know the truth."

My heart breaks for her, and I can't imagine the pain brought on by deception and betrayal.

Abandoned by the one who promised to love and to cherish until death, she is alone. Is she still a woman? All that she has known herself to be as a wife is now gone. Is she still a woman? The one with whom she had become one had given himself to another. Is she still a woman?

Three months later, we inadvertently meet again. My children and I are at the library for story time. As I enter the reading area, I see her sitting at a table, books spread out in front of her, intent upon the task at hand. Greeting her, I ask how she is doing.

"With God's strength, I'm making it," she replies with a

soft smile. She explains how she is learning to make the multitude of decisions thrust upon her. She has decided to go back to school. On this day she is studying for a test. Her face lights up as she talks about how God is meeting her needs financially, providing everything from new tennis shoes to a used car. "God's all I have now," she states with a quiet calm.

And He's enough.

Another woman, another moment, another picture of beauty.

She chose to allow God to use the broken places of her life to create something beautiful. The Holy Spirit whispers, "Speak what you see."

I see beauty.

She leans against her Savior, and she finds grace. Knowing that only God can sustain her, she stands in the face of fear and resolves not to give up. She recognizes that the things of God are the only things that matter. Seeking after the things of Christ, she lives a life of integrity. She is a fighter, a survivor, a woman of strength.

She is beauty.

HER name is beauty. The wife of a public figure, she has learned that people place high expectations on who she should be, how she should act, and how she should look. Now fifty-four, she feels increasing pressure to meet these expectations.

But she never loses the air of grace surrounding her.

Other women draw comfort from being around her. On many occasions—when I have felt lonely, inadequate, and weak—a smile or a hug from her reminds me I am loved. But it's not only her love that I feel. Her hugs and smiles reflect a greater love. Her Father's love. My Father's love.

She is my mentor, my friend, and she is beautiful. She's the kind of woman I want to be when I mature. As we quickly pass one another at church on busy Sunday mornings, I often tell her she is beautiful. She seems never to wonder who she is or where she belongs. Certainly, being the godly woman she is, she never questions her significance or her beauty. But there are days when she feels the pressure of her own expectations.

And so I tell her she is beautiful—because she is.

When I first met her almost nine years ago, I saw her as a pillar of strength, a woman whose faith remained unshaken in the face of change. Still, though, she is a woman, flesh and blood. She weeps, she laughs, she wonders, she searches, she longs.

And life changes.

Entering one of the most drastic life changes of every woman, she finds herself struggling with everyday tasks and emotions. Exhaustion overwhelms her, both physically and emotionally. She asks God when she'll feel like herself again. Some days she hears only silence.

Her emotions roil and rage. She cries. Is she still a woman? Gone are the reminders that her body could produce life. Is she still a woman? Night sweats, hot flashes—her body is not her own. Is she still a woman?

Nine years later, I still see her as a pillar of strength, a woman whose faith remains unshaken in the face of change. The Holy Spirit whispers, "Speak what you see."

I see beauty.

She leans against her Savior, and she finds grace. Knowing that only God can sustain her, she stands in the face of fear and resolves not to give up. She recognizes that the things of God are the only things that matter. Seeking after the things of Christ, she lives a life of integrity. She is a fighter, a survivor, a woman of strength.

She is beauty.

THE journey toward understanding who we are as women in Christ is simply that—a journey. Each day we live we are in the process of becoming more like Christ. Likewise, understanding our beauty through God's eyes is a journey. Each moment we face the choice of seeing ourselves through the world's eyes or through God's eyes. Many days we long for the journey's end, the place where we'll never struggle to love ourselves again. But still, not yet there, we press on.

Stops along the way change our lives. When God began healing my broken self-image, I hoped I'd never again struggle to understand my beauty. But through my own experiences, and through watching other women, I've learned that finding my beauty in Christ is a lifelong process. Some days our beauty in Christ is apparent. Other days it is engulfed in darkness, and we pray for the eyes of wisdom to help us see it—wisdom for the moment, wisdom for the future when inevitable changes will come.

In his futuristic novel *Brave New World*, Aldous Huxley pictures a society that, among other things, refuses to grow old. Seeing old age as "repulsive,"[1] the people in Huxley's world "keep [members'] secretions artificially balanced at youthful equilibrium[,] . . . give them transfusion of young blood . . .[and] keep their metabolism permanently stimulated."[2] When one woman finds herself separated from mainstream society and its artificial processes, her body goes through the natural (to us) aging process. When she returns to the brave new world where women maintain their beauty through airbrushing and synthetic stimulants, she is rejected and left to die alone, for

> nobody had the smallest desire to see Linda . . . and this was by far the strongest reason for people's not wanting to see poor Linda—there was her appearance. Fat, having lost her youth; with bad teeth, and a blotched complexion, and that figure . . . you simply couldn't look at her without feeling sick, yes, positively sick. So the best people were determined *not* to see Linda.[3]

Taking soma, a drug that produces an endless holiday from reality, Linda escapes a world that would not have her.

Written in 1932, Huxley's prediction rings true today. We vehemently reject the aging process and herald the success of those who seem to escape the physical markings of time. While few of us pursue the timeless look through face-lifts, miracle creams, and herbal remedies—or through the vibro-vac machines and wonder pills of Huxley's world—we certainly don't silence our longings to achieve eternal youth. Often, we even validate such a pursuit in our admiration for a sixty-year-old woman who maintains the appearance of a twenty-year old. We accept and reject ourselves and others based on appearance. We cannot see beyond the external. Perhaps we believe that if we cling to our worldly ideal of youth and beauty, we can become the idol of timeless beauty that we worship.

But still our breasts sag and the wrinkles appear. Life changes and our bodies change. No amount of wishing can bring back the body or face we had ten years ago, nor can any level of self-hatred bring us the body or face we've always wanted.

There exists, though, an unchanging truth.

The Lover of our souls passionately desires us. The beauty of this world will fade, but His is eternal. No amount of clothing or accessories will satisfy our longings for beauty. Our body sizes cannot reveal the depth of our true beauty. No hairstyle or physical feature is indicative of God's potential for our lives. We are chosen, called, set apart for His glory. God's destiny for our lives does not lie in some unknown, hidden place. Our destiny lies in a relationship with the One who calls us His own. Our destiny lies in the journey to know true beauty, the journey to know Him.

Women often turn to the book of Proverbs to find a detailed picture of a godly woman. Proverbs 31:10–31 is rich in its portrayal of the life and character of a woman who pursues the heart of God, but Proverbs also presents another woman of true spiritual beauty.

She is more desirable than the finest treasures (Proverbs 3:14–15). She brings happiness to those who pursue her (Proverbs 3:13), and she honors those who embrace her (Proverbs 4:7–8). Her name is Beauty. Her name is Wisdom.

Wisdom reveals to us the true definition of beauty, and through wisdom we see the baseness of the world's beauty. The world perverts what God created in purity when it tells women that beauty is defined by the ability to attain a culturally defined standard of physical perfection or by the ability to be sexually provocative. But wisdom restores purity to beauty; and it is this purity, this ability to see beyond the world, that makes wisdom's beauty so valuable, for it cannot be bought with worldly wealth.

To our detriment, the world has made sexuality and physical appearance the sum total of female identity. In the mind of God, however, women are a gift. Scripture says, "the rib which the LORD God had taken from man He made into a woman, and He *brought her to the man*" (Genesis 2:22, italics added). We were not an afterthought. Everything about us was designed by God to reflect His glory. A woman's beauty and sexuality—as purposed by God—are elements of who she is, but not the total. When we allow God to define our beauty and our sexuality, their inherent power brings life to those around us. However, when we willfully remove our beauty and our sexuality from God's intended purpose, they remain powerful but they become destructive.

We fail to realize that we do not control the power of our beauty or our sexuality when we use them outside of God's intended purpose. Using beauty and sexuality to gain power leads to slavery, not freedom; to defeat, not victory. Instead, we need to acquire the wisdom that will unlock the power of God-designed beauty and sexuality and set us free to use and enjoy them as God intended:

> Counsel is mine, and sound wisdom;
> I am understanding, I have strength.
> By me kings reign,
> And rulers decree justice.
> By me princes rule, and nobles,
> All the judges of the earth.
> I love those who love me,
> And those who seek me diligently will find me.
> (Proverbs 8:14–17)

Wisdom guides us to live out God's design for beauty, and thus wisdom enables God's power to move through us. True power comes through our pursuit of God's wisdom and beauty.

Wisdom's beauty withstands the changes of life and the passage of time: "I have been established from everlasting, from the beginning, before there was ever an earth" (Proverbs 8:23). When God spoke the world into existence, wisdom and beauty formed the foundations. Why then do we pursue the frail, broken beauty of this world?

Find Wisdom and let her teach you how to silence the voices that do not reflect the truth of who you are in Christ. Hear the voice of God as He calls you His beloved.

Find Wisdom and let her teach you to love the woman God has created you to be. Let her teach you to stand in awe and wonder at the marvelous work of God's hand when He made you.

Find Wisdom and let her teach you how to treat your body as the temple of Christ. Know that you are a sanctuary for the One who is your refuge.

Find Wisdom and let her teach you to stand in a place of proper perspective. When you seek her, she will guard your mind and transform your thoughts.

Find Wisdom and let her teach you how to allow your husband to revel in the body of the wife of his youth, not in his wife's youthful body. Let him take pleasure in the true, genuine, one-of-a-kind you—sags, bags, rolls, and all.

Find Wisdom and let her teach you that your life will change and so will your body. Let her also remind you that you serve an unchangeable God who has loved you from the beginning of time.

Wisdom calls to you. She "calls aloud outside; she raises her voice in the open squares. She cries out in the chief concourses, at the openings of the gates in the city she speaks her words" (Proverbs 1:20–21). As you pursue Christ, pursue Wisdom, for "If you seek her as silver, and search for her as for hidden treasures; then you will understand the fear of the LORD, and find the knowledge of God" (Proverbs 2:4–5). As Solomon, the wisest of all men, knew, "Charm is deceitful and beauty is passing, but a woman who fears the LORD, she shall be praised" (Proverbs 31:30).

Perhaps Solomon was alluding to words from ancient Israel's songbook: "The fear of the LORD is the beginning of wisdom; a good understanding have all those who do His commandments. His praise endures forever" (Psalm 111:10).

God does not admonish us to seek wisdom and then hide it from us. He willingly gives wisdom to those who are willing to obey His commandments. And to those who are willing to ask, God stands waiting to give us the gift of His wisdom—wisdom for the moment, wisdom for the changes, wisdom for a lifetime.

Dress for the journey. Allow His beauty to drape your body in gentle folds and His peace to be a crown upon your head. Place His wisdom upon your feet to guide each step. Finally, smile, for you do not journey alone.

An ordinary woman, she serves an extraordinary God. In her moments of greatest weakness, God reveals Himself through her. She has chosen to allow God to use the broken pieces of her life to create something beautiful. She is a pillar of strength, a woman whose faith remains unshaken in the face of change. The Holy Spirit whispers, "Speak what you see."

I see beauty.

She leans against her Savior, and she finds grace. Knowing that only God can sustain her, she stands in the face of fear and resolves not to give up. She recognizes that the things of God are the only things that matter. Seeking after the things of Christ, she lives a life of integrity. She is a fighter, a survivor, a woman of strength. She is beauty.

She is you.

LOOKING IN THE MIRROR
Personal Reflections

What changes have you experienced in your life that have affected (either positively or negatively) your understanding of beauty? Explain how each of these changes affected your self-perception.

Write the words of James 1:5.

Read James 3:17. What signs accompany the wisdom of God?

"[A]nd every gifted artisan in whom the LORD has put *wisdom* and understanding, to know how to do all manner of work for the service of the sanctuary . . ." (Exodus 36:1, italics added. For additional study, read Exodus 31:3, 6b; 35:26, 31). In the Old Testament, the tabernacle was built through the work of the Lord as He endowed the craftsmen with the wisdom of the Holy Spirit in their endeavors. The tabernacle was both a place of worship and a place of beauty. The artisans worked to build a place in which the Spirit of the Lord would dwell. While they were all skilled artisans, the key to understanding their abilities resides in the common bond they shared—they were endowed with the wisdom of the Holy Spirit. The beauty of the tabernacle was a natural result of their willingness to use their God-given gifts to worship Him. Worship in search of wisdom finds beauty. So too it is with our lives. As we seek to worship the Lord, the Holy Spirit gives us wisdom and our lives become a place of beauty, a sanctuary for the Spirit of the Living God.

Write a prayer asking God to use the broken pieces of your life to create a place of beauty, a sanctuary of worship to Him.

As you continue this journey, remember, "[B]eing confident of this very thing, that He who has begun a good work in you will complete it until the day of Jesus Christ" (Philippians 1:6).

· · · **N O T E S** · · ·

Chapter 1 | Worldly Beauty

1. Walt Mueller, YouthCulture@Today Newsletter, "What You See Is What I Am," Spring 2001, 18.

2. Stephen Crane, "I Saw a Man Pursuing," *American Literature: The Makers and the Making*, eds. Cleanth Brooks, R. W. B. Lewis, and Robert Penn Warren (New York: St. Martin's Press, 1973), 1652.

3. Mary Pipher, PhD, *Reviving Ophelia: Saving the Selves of Adolescent Girls* (New York: G. P. Putnam's Sons, 1994), 56.

4. Ibid.

5. Alex Witchel, "Everybody Loves Patricia," *Ladies Home Journal,* March 2003, 126.

6. Guthrie, Motyer, Stibbs, Wiseman. eds., *The New Bible Commentary: Revised* (Grand Rapids, Mich.: Wm. B. Eerdmans Publishing Co., 1970), 1264.

7. William Wordsworth, "The World Is Too Much with Us," *The Norton Anthology of English Literature*, Fifth Edition, ed. M. H. Abrams (New York: W. W. Norton & Co., 1986), 220.

Chapter 2 | Voices Without

1. Sandra Cisneros, *The House on Mango Street* (New York: Random House, 1984), 50–51.

Chapter 3 | Voices Within

1. Nicole Johnson, *A Fresh Brewed Life* (Nashville: Thomas Nelson Publishers, 1999), 38.

2. T. S. Eliot, "The Love Song of J. Alfred Prufrock" *American Literature: The Makers and the Making*, 2102–2103.

Chapter 4 | Mirror, Mirror

1. Nicole Johnson, *A Fresh Brewed Life*, 69.

2. F. Scott Fitzgerald, *The Great Gatsby* (New York: Simon & Schuster, 1953), 110–111.

3. Marvin Wilson, *Our Father Abraham: Jewish Roots of the Christian Faith* (Grand Rapids, Mich.: Wm. B. Eerdmans Publishing Co., 1989), 13, 15.

Chapter 5 | Idols and Temples

1. Nathaniel Hawthorne, *The Scarlet Letter* (Evanston: McDougal-Little, 1997), 225.

2. Abraham Wright, "Psalm 139," *Psalms* (Grand Rapids: Kregel Publications, 1968), 640.

Chapter 6 | A New Perspective

1. John Keats, "Ode on a Grecian Urn," *The Norton Anthology of English Literature*, 823.

2. "Identity," *Webster's Ninth New Collegiate Dictionary*, 1989 ed.

3. Guthrie, Motyer, Stibbs, Wiseman. eds., *The New Bible Commentary: Revised*, 1039–1040.

4. Emily Dickinson, "The Soul Selects Her Own Society," *American Literature: The Makers and the Making*, 1243.

Chapter 7 | Body by Charis

1. Charles Haddon Spurgeon, "Psalm 139," *Psalms*, 637.

2. Holly Robinson, "Body Blues," *Parents Magazine*, August 2002.

3. Holly Robinson, "Will I Ever Have Sex Again?" *Parents Magazine,* January 2003, 62.

4. Ibid.

Chapter 8 | A Model Figure

1. Mary Pipher, PhD, *Reviving Ophelia*, 55.

2. Mary Pipher, PhD, *Reviving Ophelia*, 40.

3. Paul Robertson, "My Trip Through *Seventeen*," YouthCulture@Today Newsletter, Fall 2002, 14–15.

4. *Cosmogirl!* April 2003.

5. *Girls Life, Magazine,* February–March 2003.

6. *Seventeen,* April 2003.

7. *Cosmogirl!* April 2003.

8. *TeenVogue,* April–May 2003.

9. *Seventeen*, April 2003.

10. *Cosmogirl!* April 2003.

11. Express Clothing, advertisement. Appeared in windows of Express Store in Augusta Mall, Augusta, Georgia, Winter 2002.

12. Express Clothing, advertisement. Appeared in windows of Express Store in Augusta Mall, Augusta, Georgia, Spring 2003.

13. *Teen People,* April 2003.

14. Paul Robertson, "My Trip Through *Seventeen*," 19.

15. Barbara Walters, *20/20*, ABC, New York, 14 February 2003, 10:00 p.m. EST.

16. Walt Mueller, "Justin and Christina: Innocence Lost or Truth Be Told?" YouthCulture@Today Newsletter, Spring 2003, 2.

17. Barbara Walters, *20/20*, ABC, New York, 14 February 2003, 10:00 p.m. EST.

18. Nicole Johnson, *A Fresh Brewed Life*, 81.

Chapter 9 | About Face

1. Aldous Huxley, *Brave New World* (New York: HarperCollins Publishers, 1946), 138.

2. Aldous Huxley, *Brave New World*, 111.

3. Aldous Huxley, *Brave New World*, 153.

NOTE TO THE READER

THE publisher invites you to share your response to the message of this book by writing Discovery House Publishers, P. O. Box 3566, Grand Rapids, MI 49501, USA. For information about other Discovery House books, music, or videos, contact us at the same address or call 1-800-653-8333. Find us on the Internet at http://www.dhp.org/ or send e-mail to books@dhp.org.